THE ANCHORS
OF DEMOCRACY

א A L E F
Series of works on universal logic and philosophy directed by
Michele Malatesta and Rocco Pezzimenti
A   Allgemeine Logik Und Philosophie
L   Universel Logik Og Filosofi
E   Logica Universale E Filosofia
F   Logica Universal Y Filosofia

Rocco Pezzimenti, *THE ANCHORS OF DEMOCRACY. A New Division of Powers, Representation, Sense of Limits*

THE ANCHORS OF DEMOCRACY

*A New Division of Powers,
Representation,
Sense of Limits*

Rocco Pezzimenti

GRACEWING

First published in 2021

Gracewing
2 Southern Avenue
Leominster
Herefordshire HR6 0QF
United Kingdom
www.gracewing.co.uk

All rights reserved. No part of this publication may be reproduced, stored in a retrieval system, or transmitted in any form, or by any means, electronic, mechanical, photocopying, recording, or otherwise, without the written permission of the publisher.

© 2021 Rocco Pezzimenti

ISBN 978 0 85244 984 4

Contents

Introduction 11

I. BUT CAN ONE REALLY EXPORT DEMOCRACY? 15

II. DEMOCRACY AND THE CULTURE OF LIMITS 21

III. LEGALITY AND THE CULTURE OF LIMITS 31

IV. ORDER AND THE SENSE OF LIMITS:
  THE ROLE OF CIVIL SOCIETY 39

V. WHICH PLURALISM? 47

VI. EDUCATING PEOPLE IN POLITICAL
  AND SOCIAL REPRESENTATION 59

  1. 'Excess of democracy' 59
  2. The fracture between society and politics and
    the implosion of the latter 61
  3. Representation and participation 66
  4. Social representation as a safeguard for political
    representation and democratic power 69
  5. Representation and responsibility:
    the delegating of authority 74

VII. TOWARDS A NEW DIVISION OF POWERS 79

  1. The tri-partition of the classic powers and new needs 80
  2. The fourth power, the fifth power and the two faces
    of the sixth power 87
  3. The transformation and the growing role of other powers 94

VIII. MORE ON THE DIVISION OF POWERS — 99

IX. THE COMMON GOOD AND ITS VALUES — 109

1. Towards a real retrieval of the common good — 109
2. Values and the common good — 111

X. THE RISE, DECLINE AND RETURN OF SOVEREIGNTY: THE CRISIS OF GROWTH — 121

1. Prior intimations of the question — 121
2. The debate during modernity and the distortions of absolutism — 125
3. The contemporary situation — 130
4. The foundations and limits of sovereignty — 134
5. The rights of the person and other limits for sovereignty — 139
6. Can one really speak about a crisis of sovereignty? — 144

XI. POLYARCHY. MULTICULTURAL AND MULTI-ETHNIC SOCIETIES: ADVANTAGES, DANGERS AND A SENSE OF LIMITS — 147

1. Polyarchy and multiculturalism — 150
2. Ethnicity: values and dangers — 155

XII. TRUTH AND DEMOCRACY: CAN ONE DO WITHOUT FOUNDATIONS? — 161

1. Between scepticism and realism — 163
2. Truth as a political question — 168
3. Truth and law: why speak about inalienable rights and conscientious objection? — 176

XIII. POPULISM AND POPULARISM — 183

1. Contemporary populism — 183
2. A recurrent temptation — 189
3. How to get out of the swamp — 192

XIV. TOWARDS HYPERDEMOCRACY? THE CRISIS
OF LIMITS 197

1. A retrospective look 197
2. In praise of representation 201
3. The reasons behind the risk of totalitarian democracy 202

Index of Names 205

INTRODUCTION

In many countries the beginning of the new millennium ended by transforming a fundamental question that had characterised the political debate of what is by now usually called modernity. More than continuing to ask how a democratic society is different from others, today it is asked what makes one society more democratic than others and how this greater degree of democracy avoids those dangerous involutions which, unfortunately, can accompany the lives of democracies.

A recurrent concern is the distancing of citizens from being concerned about the public domain, even though some observers have an untroubled attitude to this phenomenon – seeing it as something that is pathological to mature democracies. Those democracies, it should be made clear, which, in encountering an acceptance by everyone of the essential values of a certain system, can even allow a large part of the citizens to remain peripheral to institutions for a more or less long period of time, only intervening when the fundamental points of civic life are threatened. In effect, one is dealing with realities where the 'minimum' threshold of democracy has been consolidated and nobody believes that it can be called into question. But can one be satisfied with this 'minimum' threshold of democracy? Even worse, in doing this does one not run the risk of losing one of the basic elements of democracy, namely participation? Without participation and a corresponding sense of responsibility, is it still possible to speak about democracy?

These are questions that cannot be avoided because not to answer them is equivalent to accepting forms of the management of power that are near to systems of democracy where this last is masked to varying degrees. One of these is semi-populism. One certainly need not think of certain political leaders if we want to portray this. It is enough to see that even in the fiercest of political debates all the forces involved increasingly use simple – not to say simplistic – language, as well as slogans that do not foster serious and detailed political discussion but, rather, stances that involve passions and emotions. Another such system, which is no less worrying, derives from the first. Political forces, after losing contact with a certain electorate (from which suggestions, pressure, stimuli and so forth derive), latch on to lobbies, the world of the professions and various corporations in order to justify themselves: entities that are increasingly comfortable in the realities of political parties. Forces that were at one time extraneous to – not to say in contrast with – the parties, now constitute a useful support for them.

All of this not only constitutes a danger: it is also a contradiction in terms. Economic and social realities that at one time constituted a basis for democracy today run the risk of becoming parasites upon it, weighing it down rather than helping it to develop. Without mentioning the fact that members of the political classes no longer emerge from a constant and continuous selection, in the past an authentic school, but only advance if they are able to favour – in a legal way as well – these realities. This means a confusion of powers that is certainly not able to assure democratic development.

All of this is an encouragement to analyse the reasons for the weakening of the social bases of parties, and other political and social organisations, and to study new forms of participation. In other words, it leads us to reassess politics as a serious discipline of the humanities: what Guicciardini held to be a science of predictions based upon the study of precedents. This difficult science should produce a complete, lucid and cold intelligibility of events. A science that through rules leads to an acquisition of awareness of exceptions; a science able to provide to a political actor that fundamental prudence that human affairs must continuously educate people in and improve.[1] This means that politics needs schools that enable us to avoid improvisations.

---

1   Cf. M. D'addio, *Storia delle dottrine politiche*, vol. I (ECIG, Genoa, 1992), p. 308.

I. BUT CAN ONE REALLY EXPORT DEMOCRACY?

If there is one statement on which all people agree it is that democracy is first of all a cultural fact. To tell the truth, however, a conclusion of this kind is not very consequential. For the early Latin-speaking peoples of the Italian peninsula, culture, hence the term agriculture, specifically referred to the land and to everything that grew on it, under the watchful and patient eyes of those who lived on it and saw it change from nearby. '*Colere*' is the verb that referred to all of this and from this derived a sense of respect of an almost sacred kind for everything that this activity involved. It is certainly no accident that the word '*culto*' has the same root. Like, indeed, the word '*cultor*' – the cultivator who lived near a specific terrain and dedicated himself to all of this activity full-time. At one time this was not occasional, but it gradually became increasingly a full occupation and to such an extent that a farmer had to turn to others to defend himself or to engage in activities that he could no longer follow. Smith reminds us that it was specifically at this point, from this way of thinking about agriculture which completely absorbed those who practised it, that the first division of labour was born.

Culture, therefore, requires time: we could say that it has its times. Different forms of cultivation do not have the same periods of development and we could say the same about the various kinds of human activity. The ways in which a machine functions is something that we can at times learn in a short time but the same cannot be said about institutions and the respect that is due to them. Institutions are the result of a long gestation to which various generations have contributed. The Roman experience, like its Anglo-Saxon counterpart, demonstrates this fact rather well. The ancient Republic and its law were the expression of that *mores maiorum* that was slowly enriched over a number of centuries. In order to enjoy its advantages and the safety that sprang from them, one had to be immersed in that *modus vivendi* that was experienced for the whole of a lifetime. Cicero spoke about these institutions as a soul, an interior tie that bound together all citizens. For this reason, wherever these institutions arrived, apart from guaranteeing safety they did nothing else to impose themselves. Everywhere this fruitful coexistence between the *lex romana* and local law continued. The events of the trial of Jesus amply demonstrate this.

Modern liberalism was itself formed in this lineage. Montesquieu, who greatly admired Cicero, asked himself why so many scholars were unable to realise that legislation that could be excellent for one State, for another could even be deleterious. Yet the reason was simple. Legislation is not a rigorous scientific operation which if carried out in an impeccable way always produces the same results. Legislation has its own interiority, a soul (this is the meaning of *L'Esprit de Lois*) which is the outcome of a slow evolution of history, like nature itself.

The liberalism of Montesquieu here took up the belief masterfully expressed by Vico when he argued that 'things outside the natural state do not adapt to it and do not last in it'. This nature was not only that of exterior phenomena but also human nature. Not to take this undeniable assumption into account leads to a general crisis of politics. Indeed, it generates in similar circumstances a general decadence of culture, a widespread insensitivity that brings about a lack of *humanitas* and human values that in turn generates a growing cynicism and, finally, disinterest, towards politics.

If all of this could apply and applies to States that are more or less near to each other with more or less evident differences, what can be said about States located in different continents? The first can experience mutual influences and even enrich each other; the second very often start from positions of ignorance about each other, where they are not even able to understand each other. This is not only because they have different cultures but also because − as thinkers from Montesquieu to Wittfogel have observed − of different geopolitical locations that have an equal importance in the genesis and establishment of various institutions.

Today we ourselves, the heirs of this experience, seem to have suddenly lost the value and the meaning of these teachings. Yet they constitute the essence of our tradition. Why not recall here that ironic observation of Cicero about Plato's republic? It is easy to invent a republic suddenly for a city that does not exist, albeit a small one, and one that exists only in our imaginations, but we well know that the city in which we live, which is of an enormous size, has been formed through the contribution of extraordinary generations and over a long history. An equally long history was what allowed very many peoples to become integrated and not only to share, but also to gain from, the advantages that these institutions granted. Is it possible − and I repeat the point − that we, who should be the heirs to such an itinerary, have ended up by losing it?

Our beliefs seem to have been transformed into that fanaticism typical of millenarianism and into forms of that utopianism which wants to solve everything immediately, deceiving itself that it can perform miracles. But human beings are not able to perform miracles. In haste, they know only how to compromise what they knew how to construct with much hard work. This is a haste, moreover, that generates in interlocutors, who are already themselves diffident, a sense of revenge and hostility given that they feel that they have been treated with proud superiority. The point should be made clear: I have no doubt that the democratic institutions that we possess are the best that we have been able to achieve so far. Yet this does not mean that I can ignore that there is a part of humanity that does not have the same view and that the best way of understanding them is certainly not that of forcing them to accept what they have not yet adopted.

We need to have the patience to accept that very profound differences exist that we have to confront even before talking about politics and political systems. Our law grew up around the concept of the 'person', which for a long time was unknown to other cultures many of which encountered major difficulty before they understood it and assimilated it. But can one seek to have it adopted and make it seem to be crucial in those who fail to recognise it or whose assumptions of their own legal systems lie in other criteria?

Law is not a matter of abstruse argument on a par with a mysterious alchemy. It is Vico again who reminds us that wisdom in relation to law, when it is the result of historical culture, is authentic such wisdom, and to such an extent that it can be seen as an 'authentic philosophy'. It is on this terrain that a serous dialogue must be activated with the patience of the strong and not with the desire to impose, which is typical of the presuming. Force, if it really has to be used, must be used in extreme cases and anyway always where it can offer immediate, safe and shared outcomes, bearing in mind that force is not justified on its own otherwise it almost always generates highly uncontrollable phenomena.

The relations between States that are distant from each other and different are subject to a series of variables that cannot always be posited. Indeed, each State lives in a geopolitical situation that is always after a certain fashion interconnected with other neighbouring States. This means that when there is a wish to change the internal equilibriums of States, not only must one be concerned to ensure that future equilibriums are really more stable, one must also take into account that our equilibriums run the risk, after a certain fashion, of upsetting an entire geographical area. This is what has happened in the area of central Asia.

There are those who argue that the lack of compensations and the imbalances that have occurred in this area are also due to a series of 'cures', often of a radical kind, imposed by extraneous models, specifically as happened, for example, during the last century. Communism, Islamic fanaticism and Western outlooks followed one another in imposing themselves in a violent way. All of this took place without taking into account that a society that is in part primitive, but whatever the case characterised by a backward, and in its own way wise, equilibrium, had to be helped to grow slowly without being brutally pushed by external forces that were often in contrast with each other. In this way, governments followed one another that were friends of the Soviets and then of the Americans – governments, whatever the case, unable to keep international agreements not only with other executives but also with multinational companies. The cases of Afghanistan and Pakistan provide ample testimony of this.

On can say that the situation of the Central Asian area constitutes one of the most intricate political knots of the twenty-first century. The future equilibriums of this area, the Russian world and the Chinese world make up an authentic unknown. However, the outcomes will not fail to have consequences for the rest of the world, as the current crisis in Iraq demonstrates. But this could be a simple piece in a much broader problem. One need only remember that from those who study crisis areas there has emerged the hypothesis that the 'endurance' of the Russian world would be to the advantage of the whole of Europe. It is said that this would lead to a change of alliances and to a further extension of European institutions towards the East. However, this is a restrictive way of looking at a problem which in affecting China and India as well would end up by having not only Asian dimensions but also repercussions for the Pacific area.

The complexity of the phenomenon should not only lead us not to act in a rash way: it should also encourage us to assess it from a broader spatial-temporal point of view. Foreign policy requires the greatest prudence shorn of extemporising and supported by far-sightedness. Here, as well, the philosophical and political lesson of our tradition should after a certain fashion be of some help. Amongst others, the American Federalists themselves well knew that foreign policy expresses the permanent interests of a nation – those that concern the various generations: interests, therefore, that should not only be defended and protected but also assured so that they are made as stable as possible. To achieve this, it is necessary to eliminate those contrasts that can generate future wars, misunderstandings or, even worse, forms of hatred that produce only perennial uncertainty

II. DEMOCRACY AND THE CULTURE OF LIMITS

There has been a great deal of talk in the contemporary world about the difference that exists between the freedom of the ancients and the freedom of the moderns. This has often involved losing sight of the concrete aspects of freedom. Too much emphasis has been placed on this difference, forgetting those consequences that have always characterised freedom. One need only consider that in the view of some people we can perceive 'three cases of freedom that belong to the catalogue of freedom of the moderns or contemporaries. The *first* is the paradigmatic case of religious freedom. The *second*, that of economic freedom. The *third* that of political freedom'.[2] I believe that at least two of these three cases of freedom (but perhaps also the third) were already present in the Roman outlook, however most of the time ignored by those who speak about the ancient world, as I demonstrate elsewhere.[3] However, it now seems to me that the question that should really be stressed is another.

I. Berlin, whose contribution to the analysis of these questions was certainly one of the most original of the last century, speaks to us about negative liberty (defined by Bobbio, amongst others, as *freedom from*) and positive

---

2 S. Veca. *Dell'incertezza. Tre meditazioni filosofiche* (Feltrinelli, Milan, 1997), p. 145.

3 Cf. R. Pezzimenti, *The Open Society and its Friends, with Letters from Isaiah Berlin and Karl R. Popper* (Gracewing, Leominster, 2011).

liberty (defined as *freedom to*).[4] The first is provided by that domain within which a person must be allowed to do or not to do what he is able to do without others interfering. The second belongs, on the other hand, to that domain in which the source of control or interference can act to ensure that one thing rather than another is done. The freedom of the moderns, which should be that of the first, depends upon this difference.

'It appears that what is required by the freedom of the moderns and what is required by the freedom of the ancients is destined cyclically to enter into conflict, requesting of the political order and its rules and institutions intrinsically unstable solutions in terms of equilibrium'.[5] I feel that I should affirm that in the political contest, with certain assumptions remaining, these unstable equilibriums should be seen as congenital to freedom, as long as they do not end up by drawing it into crisis or injuring it. However, before analysing this statement a basic clarification is required.

The two terms, given what it rightly suggested by Veca and given the relational and interactive character of the context in which social freedom is described, tend to exclude the noun 'freedom' and to replace it with the adjective 'free'. The latter, as we are reminded by a long Western tradition, tends to express itself in a legal concept as a result of which each individual relates to others in the community to which he belongs.[6] Only in this way does a person agree to live in a context of shared rules, outside of which an individual is an authentic outlaw.

---

4 Cf. I. Berlin, *Four Essays on Liberty* (Oxford University Press, Oxford, 1969); Italian edition: *Quattro saggi sulla libertà* (Feltrinelli, Milan, 1997), pp. 185ff.

5 S. Veca, *Dell'incertezza. Tre meditazioni filosofiche*, p. 135.

6 Cf. *ibid.*, pp. 135-139.

Although it is easy to agree with what has just been affirmed, some consequences become more complex. In the view of some, indeed, we are free 'only if freedom is protected against violation and oppression by an *extraneous* force, which thanks to its own strength is recognised as such within the group or community'.[7] This a correct observation but it is not exhaustive. I believe, indeed, that freedom in some cases has to be 'defended' against the claims of its own strength, recognised as such within the group or community, because, as history has amply demonstrated, a force that is authorised, even by the majority, could impose on individuals choices that after a certain fashion injure their freedom. All of this means that every force, including legitimate force, encounters limits beyond which it cannot proceed, even though the majority of citizens may want this. Otherwise, with what courage could we speak about the inalienable rights of the person?

It is the concept of limits that takes away all of its abstractions from freedom and confers dignity upon freedom. Limits, indeed, apply to every expression of freedom: the freedom of the individual and the freedom of institutions and powers. Now these limits, as regards their historical character, or it would be better to say in the long term, appear as sorts of solutions that have intrinsically unstable equilibriums, but in the short term they give to the social system those certainties without which it would be impossible to live. Moreover, in their essence these limits constitute a bulwark against those principles which, once they have been undermined (I am thinking here of that of the person), run the risk of throwing every form of coexistence into crisis. One of the first limits on which our civilisation is based is provided by the fact that political rights cannot, notwithstanding their fundamental importance, be seen as

---

7   *Ibid.*, p. 139.

unique and exhaustive. This is a temptation that is always recurrent and to which modernity, as well, cannot say that it is immune. In other words, sociality is such that no political dimension can cover it in its entirety and therefore in addition to the rules of politics there should also be kept present, as Montesquieu would tell us, the rules of intermediary bodies and civil society.

Whatever the case, there remains the fact, which has been valid since the Italic peoples, whoever seeks to express it and wherever it is expressed, that 'freedom lies in laws, in the voluntary acceptance of rules established by common agreement'.[8] These rules can be changed only by consensus and as long as this is the case they cannot be transgressed by anyone.

In our cultural tradition, on which one should dwell, the 'sacredness' of these rules has always extended to relationships between individuals as well.[9] One need only think of a contract that guarantees the certainty and the self-sufficiency of one's own goods and establishes their limits in relation to third parties and the state. These limits (*termines*) had a sacral value for the early Latin-speaking peoples of the Italian peninsula that could not be discussed arbitrarily. To these *termines* were even dedicated holy feast days – the famous *terminalia*.

On this conception of limits was based the classic idea of the Republic, referred to on a number of occasions in the various experiences of past centuries. The institution of the republic lasted for such a long time precisely because it applied the concept of limits to 'class relations' as well. It was called, with a happy insight, an 'aristocratic Republic'.

---

8   J. Gaudemet, 'Il miracolo romano', in F. Braudel (ed.), *Il mediterraneo* (Bompiani, Milan, 1992), p. 172.

9   I here take up some of the points made in my already cited work *The Open Society and its Friends, with Letters from Isaiah Berlin and Karl R. Popper*.

If the people and the aristocracy did not find a synthesis, they encountered irremediable conflict. As Guicciardini acutely understood, the Republic synthesised the needs of equality and freedom: it tempered the mania for change of a people always directed to the present and the immediate future and shook the aristocracy from a selfishness that always aimed at the past looking forward to a distant future. To sum up, the aristocratic Republic ensured that changes, which were always necessary, took place with continuity and not with extemporaneousness. It based order on certainty and changeability, avoiding dangerous leaps in the dark.

All of this was possible because the two crucial 'classes' of the Roman world mutually limited each other, assuring consensus to the people and tradition to the aristocracy. The People and the Senate in their turn limited the Consuls, bringing about that mutual limitation that is the basis of our democracies. It is a pity that in a great deal of public debate the word 'limit' has acquired a meaning of negativity because in this term is contained all the positivity of true democracy which – and this is no accident – enters into crisis when it no longer considers its limits.

One of the most sensitive and also the least considered limits is rooted in the conscience of the person, by which each individual engages in interior research, discovers his desires, and gives a meaning to his expectations. The conscience is the most serious bulwark there is against any kind of irrationality and barbarity. No human authority can legislate within it. If you go beyond that limit, as Seneca warned, all distinctions between slaves and free men disappears, and in this madness only martyrdom for freedom can restore meaning to human dignity. One well understands why, in order to know how to defend that limit, again in the view of Seneca, one has even to learn to defeat the fear of dying. A situation incapable of keeping institutions within their limits leads to such extremes. Extreme cases, it will be said, but into which one inadvertently slides when one begins to systematically violate the law or to ensure that suspensions for exceptional cases become the norm. Law and the force of law are replaced by other forms of force, which are not necessarily violent but are pressures of various kinds that attract many to by-pass the law in order to achieve their own goals. One historian of the crisis of the ancients, more than blaming the barbarians, or the economic crisis, or the new religion, even though he was a pagan, relates to us the dismay of certain magistrates who were the victims of a situation that made them powerless. They were honest judges who often witnessed the truth being overturned in front of their very eyes as adventurers set fire to sentences and books of various kinds, demonstrating that barbarity typical of any people that loses its sense of limits.[10]

St. Augustine, who lived through this crisis and analysed it, was well aware that in order to move out of that uncertainty it was necessary to return to the domain of rules because peace itself is possible not when a vision of a Hobbesian character is actuated but only when a return is made to limits established by the law. The whole of medieval public debate, which found in John of Salisbury one of its highest expressions,[11] analyses authority not in a general sense but in relation to the limits to the exercise of authority itself. It is no accident that it was specifically in this period that the distinction between the public and the private, the lay and the ecclesiastical, was rediscovered – a distinction that

---

10　Cf. Ammianus Marcellinus, *Rerum Gestarum Libri Qui Supersunt* (William Heinemann LDT, London – Harvard University Press, Cambridge, Massachusetts, MCMXXXIX), XXIX, 42.

11　Cf. my *The Open Society and its Friends, with Letters from Isaiah Berlin and Karl R. Popper*, chap. IV.

would lead to the rebirth of a series of liberal professions entrusted to lay people.

From here also began the rediscovery of those limits to which any power must be subjected: limits that are not only juridical but also temporal and even respectful of that interiority which in the view of some did not exist in the period indicated. If such was not the case, why would reference have been made to the killing of tyrants? One should not forget that this extreme form was preceded by a whole series of other forms of disobedience that anybody could rightly invoke if they felt that they could not carry out certain tasks. All of this means that the political dimension could not fully absorb the lives of individuals and that the conscience constituted the extreme limit and bulwark of freedom. It is certainly no accident that Acton believed that Thomas Aquinas was the first to be able provide a Whig theory of politics and revolution.[12] But we are not only dealing with St. Thomas: numerous other theoreticians, such as Marsilius or Ockham, remind us that monarchical power itself had to respond to the grand electors who had elected it. One had, that is to say, a mandate under certain conditions that limited the power of monarchy and made it an institution that was from many points of view different to that of the modern epoch. One should not forget, for example, that Ockham circumscribed political authority within precise limits of consent, without which it had no legitimacy to govern.

What is most interesting is that this idea of limits reopened that debate about equality and freedom, which was obviously gradually improved, that was at the base

---

12   Cf. *Ibid.*, chap. V, § 19. It should be remembered that contrary to what was argued by a great deal of public debate, as early as the high Middle Ages it was impossible to be saved if one was forced to be saved. St. Augustine observed that the God that created us without us wanting this cannot save us without us wanting to be saved.

of modern discourse about democracy and liberalism. In essential terms, if these two terms have coexisted in what has opportunely been called an additive perspective,[13] this is specifically because they have discovered and valued their own and each other's limits, which tend to harmonise and not to fragment. The additive perspective envisages a sort of happy and effective 'division of labour' that also allows the denunciation of vices, failings and not kept promises,[14] without by this drawing into crisis the cardinal points on which civil coexistence is founded. A further proof of this is that an authentic democratic society has by now adopted the cultural and political perspective of limits. Indeed, only in this way is it possible to make values that at times are in conflict coexist in the belief that the *culture of limits* is able to resolve conflicts in a peaceful way and within the same rules on which the concept of limits rests. Moreover, if these rules are inadequate the culture of limits itself has to be able to change them without radically changing the framework of reference of democratic life. This is the essence of an open society which finds in respect for limits and the possibility of changing them peacefully its precondition; indeed I would say its *conditio sine qua non*.[15]

The modern sense of limits has been confirmed by its relationship with constitutionalism, even though I do not agree with those who argue that liberalism is intrinsically constitutionalism.[16] The experience of the Romans in ancient history and the experience of the British in the modern experience demonstrate the opposite. Modern

---

13   Cf. S. Veca, *Dell'incertezza. Tre meditazioni filosofiche*, p. 157.

14   Cf. *ibidem*.

15   It should be remembered that Popper argued that one of the characteristics of democracy is that it changes those who govern without the shedding of blood.

16   Cf. S. Veca, *Dell'incertezza. Tre meditazioni filosofiche*, p. 160.

constitutionalism, like ancient constitutionalism for that matter, has expressed the attempt, which historical experience transformed into necessity, to place conflicts, contrasts and discussions of various kinds within previously established limits that cannot be easily eluded. Indeed, the truth is that every constitution established special procedures to change what I have defined as its own *culture of limits*.

All of this involves some important considerations: first amongst them, moving out of our selfish presumption that our position is privileged compared to the other who with his position constitutes, in his turn, a limit that I have to take into account whatever the circumstances. The *second* belief is that from a sense of limits springs a sort of hierarchy of rules in which the more it is highlighted the more the limit is stable and difficult to undermine. In other words, the rules of consensus become more ironlike. The *third*, which is apparently unfashionable, is that a limit, in addition to being by now an aspect of life of civil life that cannot be eliminated, constitutes an essential part of the common good that is often ill-treated but which one can absolutely not do without.

III. LEGALITY AND THE CULTURE OF LIMITS

The concept of limits at a political level does not only relate to freedom – it also relates to all the fundamental requirements of civil coexistence, for example tolerance. It has been rightly observed that 'to be in favour of tolerance *without* limits is to be in favour of something different from tolerance, however interpreted'.[17] Everybody can admit that in the domain of tolerance the intolerant have no place. They want to impose their own truth believing that they possess a monopoly on truth.

Tolerance, in the view of Popper, should be exercised towards all those who are not intolerant and this means that one should treat every decision with respect unless it is in contrast with the very principle of tolerance.[18] Popper feels that he has to make some additions to this perhaps rather restrictive logical distinction. Indeed, when speaking about the *paradoxes of democracy* after the paradoxes *of tolerance*, he identifies the paradox of majority government. On the basis of this principle one could present the possibility that the majority decides to entrust government to a tyrant, that is to say to an intolerant man.[19] These possible and undeniable distortions cannot,

---

17 S. Veca, *Dell'incertezza. Tre meditazioni filosofiche*, p. 207.
18 f. K. R. Popper, *The Open Society and its Enemies*, vol. I, *The Spell of Plato* (Routledge and Kegan Paul, London and Henley, 1977), p. 235, note 6.
19 Cf. *Ibid.*, p. 265, note 4.

however, make us forget the benefits of tolerance which remains, of itself, a good.

This belief, even though today it seems to be an evident aspect of very many liberal and democratic realities, implies another danger that must not be neglected. The political authorities and institutions that should guarantee tolerance can run the risk of becoming intolerant and end up in various ways imposing their own positions which are held to be more just and more true than others. Yet this is not the only risk: imposition in some cases can be as equally damaging as neutrality in others.

Defending the fundamental principles of civil life must become an inalienable criterion that cannot allow indecisions. Allowing citizens to take part in political life in order to enjoy the rights of citizenship must be an inalienable fact, like eliminating all the obstacles that stand in the way of this goal. Intolerance, indeed, is certainly one of these. In relation to such subjects, the authorities can hold themselves to be neither neutral nor even too invasive. The saying of Terentius, '*nihil humanum a me alienum esse puto*', should be revisited by dwelling upon the word '*humanum*'. In this case we would understand that intolerance cannot be seen as human like that neutrality that makes us close our eyes to variously expressed offences against humanity.

In order to actuate such a conviction, the various political institutions should have the *humility* to take a step backwards and recognise that certain rights, acknowledged as belonging to *humanum* or even better to *humanitas*, are above individual States or certain alliances between States and belong to humanity in general. This conviction is today finally becoming universal. Its 'reasonableness' is separate from philosophical disputes, rather like those principles of classical law which, although at times not implemented, cannot be said by anyone to be erroneous. One may think here of the famous '*honeste vivere, alterum non laedere, suum cuique tribuere*'.[20]

The idea has increasingly gained ground that transgressing those limits, which are at the base of civil life so understood, do not lead to practical disorder alone, given that there are repercussions at the level of thought as well, and thus in the interiority of man. From here was born the need for law. Indeed, if there had been the certainty that limits would never have been transgressed, rules to uphold them and protect them would not have been produced.

Law thus emerges as one of the instruments of control and thus of rationalisation of life in order to avoid disorder. This sense of limits constitutes the source of social concord. Indeed, to such an extent that it is a fact that society in general, like particular societies, will last 'as long as the members persevere in their agreement',[21] that is to say as long as they accept the limits that have been given or until they decide to change them on the basis of commonly accepted rules.

But whence arises the agreement about commonly accepted limits? Ulpian reminds us of an assumption on which one should reflect. He tells us that jurisprudence finds its *raison d'être* in separating 'what is right from what is not right, distinguishing the licit from the illicit'.[22] The law becomes, that is to say, the discriminating criterion; the *limit*, indeed, in the domain in which one practises one's own freedom. Without this limit, freedom itself disappears because it no longer knows what to anchor itself in and how to assure its existence. This is the crucial task of the State. *Politics must guarantee a sense of limits and must guarantee*

---

20 *Digest*, 1,1,10.
21 Gaius, *Institutionis* (Ed. Quattro Venti, Urbino, 1994), III, 148-151.
22 *Digest*, 1,1,1.

its change in the domain of legality. If the opposite is the case, nobody can feel guaranteed. As a classical writer said: 'No man has a private position so solid that it does not fall into ruin if the State fails; in contrary fashion, a happy State provides a remedy to the misfortunes of its citizens'.[23] It is obvious here that by the State is meant the guarantee of legality, the expression of that *ubi societas ibi ius* without which certainty no longer exists and coexistence becomes a setting of extemporisation and insecurity.

Certainly this is not only a question of rights, which whatever the case remain an inescapable point of departure. One is dealing, however obvious this may be, with reformulating pluralism itself, which is too often held to be formal or, even worse, abstract. Reference has never been made to pluralism more than it is today, but never before has it been so offended. More than affirming concrete respect for people, reference has been made to respect for ideas and those who have made themselves their bearers in the most offensive and bestial ways have condemned themselves. In contrary fashion, ideas can be discussed and combatted in the most suitable ways not least because the minimum we can say of some of them is that they are unacceptable. Without, however, forgetting the greatest respect for those who are their bearers. This is the only pluralism that does not lose from sight the concreteness of life.

Concrete pluralism leads us to read anew the management itself of conflict which, when it takes place in the domain of legality, can be an inexhaustible source of improvement. This means developing what some define as authentic ethics of conflict which, understood in these terms, can become an authentic *social value*. Developing ethics of conflict (which I prefer to call *ethics of competitive dialogue*), given the

---

23 Cassius Dio, *Roman History*, vol. III (William Heinemann LDT, London – The MacMillan Co., New York, MCMXIV), XXXVIII, 36,8.

inability of every juridical system to be seen as complete and definitive, assures the possibility of change in a way that respects the plurality of opinions and above all the plurality of individuals who support it. All of this involves nobody ever having to be obliged to abandon the legitimacy of the cause for which they fight, unless this cancels or endangers the beliefs of other people. Only in this way is respect for minorities assured and majorities are constantly led to believe that their positions, in addition to not being exhaustive, are *also the outcome* of the need to have to take decisions. This is the element that constitutes the fulcrum of politics.

Another fundamental assumption follows from this: the ongoing dialogue that sustains the possibility of that *conversion* that not only has a relevance at a political level but at a social level as well tends to make it mature and deepen. To some people all of this could even seem – because it is continuous and frenetic – a ridiculous pursuit of novelty that has little to do with the deepening of one's own beliefs. However, these people should remember the true sense of conversion. 'Conversion also means persevering in a moral decision that was previously taken, persevering in a dimension that always has the character of a beginning, thus of the new in relation to the natural *continuum*'.[24] This is a right that belongs to every person and in this domain everyone must uphold the right not to be deceived by another person.

This, too, is another right that cannot be eliminated in relationships between people. There is no rightly understood right that can defend false promises. Indeed, law can

---

24 R. Spaemann, *Versuche über den Unterschied zwischen 'etwas' und 'jemand'* (Nachfolger GmbH, Stuttgart, 1998); Italian edition: *Persone. Sulla differenza tra 'qualcosa' e 'qualcuno'* (Laterza, Bari-Roma, 2005), pp. 207-208.

oblige a person to keep promises that are formulated in the right way. 'Forgetting a promise does not invalidate the obligation to keep it. It should not be forgotten. A right does not become extinguished if its possessor does not remember it...in promising, we forgo a part of ourselves, we grant to another a right over us'.[25] If such were not the case, no community, or human consortium, could survive. Not only would the implementation of promises not be assured. The same applies even to the freedom to make them, and, with this, one of the essential aspects of freedom: *generosity*.

With the loss of generosity, there occurs also the loss of one of the fundamental requirements of intelligence – enthusiasm. Intellectuals no longer risk, they do not invent, they no longer raise critical voices. They adapt to a cultural reality that becomes increasingly uniform and marked by scandalmongering, one that is scarcely original and therefore unable to promote progress. Culture looks for market products and it, too, moves towards becoming an expression of an industrialism that has invaded every aspect of human life. This danger was perceived by Tocqueville himself with words that are of as much contemporary relevance as they have ever been: 'Democracy not only infuses a taste for letters among the trading classes, but introduces a trading spirit into literature. In aristocracies, readers are fastidious and few in number; in democracies, they are far more numerous and far less difficult to please. The consequence is, that among aristocratic nations, no one can hope to succeed without immense exertions, and that these exertions may bestow a great deal of fame, but can never earn much money; whilst among democratic nations, a writer may flatter himself that he will obtain at a cheap rate a meagre reputation and a large fortune. For this purpose he need not be admired; it is enough that he is

---

25   *Ibid.*, p. 218.

liked'.[26] These authors, in the pursuit of money and success, increasingly multiply and 'for some few great authors... you may reckon thousands of idea-mongers'.[27]

It is certainly the case that we should not have a nostalgic attitude towards an aristocratic system that was much marked by other faults. However, we should see the negative consequences of a culture, consequences that can be reduced in size by increasing a sound basic culture that deepens that sense of limits that can provide to culture, as well, rigorousness and a respect for limits and thus for man. Otherwise all we can do is to adapt to a scandal-mongering mentality which, pursuing the new at any cost, sees (although it would be better to say 'wants') certain progress, when, in fact, it is not such.

Every action or choice in politics must posit ambivalent outcomes. As Guicciardini reminds us, antilogies are the real meaning of political action and, even before that, of choices. This explains why even the best intentions can flounder. Tocqueville, even though he was an undoubted democratic spirit and believed in equality, ended his work by warning: 'The nations of our times cannot prevent the conditions of men from becoming equal; but it depends upon themselves whether the principle of equality is to lead them to servitude or freedom, to knowledge or barbarism, to prosperity or wretchedness'.[28] There is no doubt that the positive elements of these dichotomies are based upon this sense of limits which has to be cultural in order to be legal.

It is these positive elements that must be defended and encouraged. To be afraid of the negative means losing the

---

26 A. de Tocqueville, *Democracy in America*, translated by Henry Reeve, with an *Introduction* by Joseph Epstein, vol. I and II (A Bantam Classic, New York, 2000), p. 577.

27 *Ibid.*, p. 577.

28 *Ibid.*, p. 888.

most hidden meaning of democracy – that of improving itself continuously by controlling negative tendencies and various forms of pessimism. The dialectic between the positive and the negative cannot sterilise a process that, with evil, also runs the risk of cancelling what good has been arduously achieved. We should embrace the conclusion of Tocqueville on freedom of the press – an aspect that offers dangers and demagogic possibilities that can be easily imagined and are difficult to control but which also has enormous positive potential that would disappear if censorship were introduced. Thus the dangers exist but the advantages are far greater and for this reason every individual must defend freedom of the press, and with it its positive aspects.

IV. ORDER AND THE SENSE OF LIMITS: THE ROLE OF CIVIL SOCIETY

The word 'order', after the event of the twentieth century, sounds a little 'strange' in the ears of those who are interested in politics. Governments that made themselves the paladins of order offered a precise approach, with characteristics of a blind imposition and, whatever the case, always of authoritarianism. And yet, to see things aright, in these cases reference is made to an imposed and authoritarian order which is the exact opposite of what is intended by democratic order, which is an order of legality.

Those who are nostalgic for this purported 'lost' order often sigh, remembering that 'one could leave home with the door open' or that 'the trains always ran on time'. I confess that I have never understood why in a democracy trains could not run on time.

Behind the apparent banality, a problem of this kind harbours rather important motivations: a society, rightly understood, implies a will that actuates a real process of unification of the individuals that make it up.[29] It is obvious that this will refers to the nature of the ends that justify associated life, a will not of society, as we understand it today, but of the political body. The difference is necessary above all now when today's politics, with the international context, internal impulses, migration flows, and economic and financial convulsions, has to learn to immerse itself in the differences of will and re-emerge

---

29 Cf. M. D'Addio, *Storia delle dottrine politiche*, p. 144.

with a solution that is, as much as possible, shared. There emerges from this, therefore, a will that is the expression of a dynamic order.

The State finds a foundation in this process otherwise it would be a structure extraneous to the social body. This process of unification characterises the order of a society. All of this means that political society and the order that corresponds to it cannot be generated from a static reality because everything in the political dimension is seen in constant dynamism. Indeed, every institution is the expression of the most complex existential impulses of human beings, including vices and virtues.

This explains why everything in politics, including peace and social justice, can be continually improved but is also continually threatened. This means that the political order, albeit with its dynamic quality, 'has to be continually willed'. When this will is lost, 'the order disintegrates from within, when the processes of decadence [those that make trains run late normally and habitually] of a political society mature in its deepest strata and are not immediately perceivable'.[30] Society, therefore, disintegrates from within, at its inner will, and is no longer able to support the motivations that established it.

Here it would be appropriate to refer to that latent tension that Kant defined as 'unsociable sociability' (which I feel is the fitting translation of the German *ungesellige gesellichkeit* despite other translations in a series of languages). This, beyond being an innovation, belongs to the best tradition of the West. One need only remember the very happy phrase of Lucan – *concordia discors*[31] – which underlay a basic belief of Roman jurisprudence.

30　*Ibidem*. The text in squared brackets is mine.
31　Lucan, *The Civil War* (William Heinemann LDT, London – G. P. Putnam's Sons New York, MCMXXVIII), I, 98.

Order and sociality cannot by their nature be taken for granted. On the contrary: human nature needs laws and customs in order to express what in all likelihood is only a tendency. If such was not the case, order and legality could never be endangered. Rather, they have to be continually willed because they could run the risk of floundering. As Seneca told Nero, power must seek to assure and not to overwhelm; force must exist for a regulated and peaceful order that otherwise would not exist. Outside this approach, power itself becomes too great, no longer has limits, becomes insatiable, and on a par with certain passions ends up by no longer having rules.[32] In this case, you no longer have good government because order is the outcome of a simple imposition and not of a relationship between the parties based on consensus.

From what has been said above, it emerges that order, like peace or social justice, is a painful search of humanity and can never be said to have been acquired once and for all. History, here, does not perform miracles or even offer gifts, not least because the boundary between an order that rightly must, and can, be modified in continuity, and the mania to change everything immediately, cannot be easily established *a priori*. Often the dramatic consequences appear clear only *a posteriori*. One should be careful, therefore, about rejecting or dismissing too hurriedly order based, obviously, upon legality, because it constitutes the pre-supposition of every political institution that wants to improve itself and not destroy itself. Here one is dealing with what classical authors defined as *tranquillitas ordinis*, which had a value that went beyond a mere interior meaning, even if this enables

---

[32] Cf. L. A. Seneca, 'De Clementia', in *Moral Essays*, vol. I (William Heinemann LDT, London – Harvard University Press, Cambridge Massachusetts, MCMLXX), I, 7.

us to understand that order has its interiority that lies in the consciousness of those who make up a society. One is dealing with the umpteenth demonstration that political crises are always the mirror of an existential crisis – a crisis, one could say, that begins within and then explodes without.

A serious analysis of law through its history and the way it relates to society could be a confirmation of all of this. However, it is certainly the case that one should abandon so-called 'case studies', which have always been a 'deforming malady' in some scholars of law. To study law, indeed, is almost to engage in a hermeneutic effort to understand the motivations that determined the development of a State and its decadence. This was well grasped – even though nobody remembers this anymore – by Dante himself. For this thinker, 'whoever aims at the good of the State, aims at the purpose of law. And the demonstration of this is the following: law is a real and personal relationship between one man and another, which, when maintained, maintains human society and, when corrupt, corrupts it'.[33]

At the beginning of modernity, order became the criterion that had to temper the claims of equality and freedom, which when abandoned to themselves would have ended up by compromising each other in an often irretrievable way. Indeed, wanting to absolutise one of these two terms would involve almost the total reduction of the other. In addition, order allows politics to understand with greater readiness all those innovations which, in a chaotic dimension, would end up by being underestimated or not understood in their real range. But above all else, order allows dialogue between the parties because in politics no party can be solely and fully right. Politics is in itself ambivalent, that is to say based on antilogies, and this means that every situation

---

33 Dante Alighieri, *Monarchia* (Garzanti, Milan, 1985), II, 5.

can be assessed from two different positions that are often complementary and almost never exhaustive.[34]

It is clear that in the case of a relationship between different parties involved in political competition, order becomes fundamental in assuring equivalent possibilities and conditions to both parties that foster the mutual respect of the parties in competition and rules that regulate competition itself. This is possible when my rights become for me duties towards the other. It is no accident that Gandhi could state that all the rights that have to be served and preserved come from a well performed duty.[35] For this reason, above all those great spirits that have engaged in politics animated by a strong religious sense have often contradicted a political authority that, with the excuse of maintaining a certain order, imposed a way of seeing the world that was the domination by one party of another, reduced to total silence. This is not the political order to which the wills of everybody with respect for rules should contribute, a dynamic order that springs from certain pre-suppositions that cannot be abandoned such as inalienable rights, but, rather, a static and imposed order that forgets the pre-requisite of the *consensus iuris*.

The subject of consensus refers to that of freedom, which is certainly fundamental, but one would commit a major error, and often such an error is committed, to see it as the only aspect that a political order should take into account. It is true that a certain libertarian culture moves in this direction, but an authentic political order can certainly not ignore other demands such as equality, justice and

---

34 Cf. F. Guicciardini, 'Ricordi', in R. Palmarocchi (ed.), *Scritti politici e Ricordi* (Laterza, Bari, 1931), sez. 2ª, 213, p. 334. For the relationship between equality and freedom cf. 'La decima scalata' in *Discorsi del reggimento di Firenze*.

35 Cf. M. Gandhi, in UNESCO, *Human Rights: Comments and Interpretations* (Allan Wingate, London, 1949), p. 18.

even morality,[36] which must have the same qualification of importance in order to give real credibility and dynamism to the political order.

We are thus faced with another factor that can bring about the disintegration of a political system: privileging one political prerogative over others, as libertarians do with freedom, can create strong imbalances and evident discontent. The same applies to justice which, when carried to extremes, brings about that 'justicialism' that can be the worst of all remedies, or to equality which can end up by killing merit. It is certainly no accident that some classical authors spoke about *aequabilitas*,[37] namely equality before the law, but not planning.

For there to be an ordered and dynamic balance between the various elements that constitute the basis of a political system, there should also be a balance of powers. This statement may seem a platitude, above all in a tradition such as ours, and yet such is not the case. Not only because often, in the recent past as well, as was highlighted dramatically by the twentieth century, one power has prevailed over another, but also because in a complex world such as ours the division of powers and their ordered equilibrium certainly cannot not occur and be completed in the classic tri-partition.

Indeed, there are further powers, many of which are even well 'camouflaged', that weigh upon the political order more than may be supposed and they orientate it in specific directions that do not always have a real consensus. The contemporary political order must therefore reconsider the classic powers in order to make them respond to current needs but it must also balance them with other powers that have

---

[36] Cf. on this point V. Possenti, *Le ragioni della laicità* (Rubbettino Editore, Soveria Mannelli, 2007).

[37] On this point see my *The Open Society and its Friends, with Letters from Isaiah Berlin and Karl R. Popper*, point 1, 35.

been formed and which, enjoying almost an immunity, do not respect the fundamental criterion of the division of powers. It is certainly the case today that the three classic powers deserve to be revisited in the light of the innovations that have taken place in the domain of a reality that has become increasingly complex and in need of new rules. The *legislative* power must take into account requests relating to a renewed criterion of representation. The *judicial* power must face up to cultures and moralities, and this to laws, that cannot be ignored even if they often deserve to be regulated in a suitable way. The *executive* has to meet a growing need to give – rapidly – responses that are able to direct and implement decisions. A power, that is to say, that is able to take on responsibilities and respond to the unpostponable request to render efficient the bureaucratic power, which is a fundamental support for traditional powers, in order to meet the needs of an economic world that has become marked by high speed.

But we should place at the side of the three classic powers – so that in addition to the weight that they exercise they may have precise rules and roles – those powers that have gradually become established in modernity, in order to avoid that they, too, going beyond their limits, come to occupy spaces that fall to other powers. I am alluding to the *fourth* and *fifth powers*: the press and in general the mass media and means of communication. The *sixth power* or *cybernetic* power, whose role is progressively growing and from certain points of view provoking concern, should have the same criterion of transparency.

To these I would add the need to review some of the more traditional powers which hitherto have been thought of as being often immune from controls. I am thinking of *commercial* power. Who can deny that *business* often has an enormous weight in the political affairs of the modern State? Very precise limits are required for this power as well, obviously of a political nature. An eighth power, closely connected with the previous one, is the *power of banking and finance*, whose meanders are often mostly hidden but whose importance nobody can doubt. The conflicts of interest present in this power go beyond national interests and often elude rules and controls. From this emerges the non-negotiable need to discipline some economic relationships not only in domestic politics.

And what should we say about *trade union* power, whose historic role, like its slow crumbling due to an increasingly precarious unity, cannot be doubted? Its influence should also be considered and regulated on a par with the other powers in order to avoid risks of invasiveness. A final power, which has too often been neglected and frequently thought to be dead but is always revitalised, deserves to be remembered: corporative or neo-corporative power, depending on which term one wants to use. Its ganglions are so present in civil society that it brings about choices and often ends that are at times not universally accepted.

One could flank these powers, where one should speak about a new division, by other intermediate powers which, from time to time, take on different meanings and influence. It is from this point of view that one must achieve a new political order free from all utopian contents and distant from all illusions.

As can be understood, we are dealing with a problem that is posing new challenges to political theory and practice. It is wise not to fall into the error of underestimating or postponing the problems, gripped, as we are, unfortunately, by a contingent dimension that above all in politics does not seem to leave room for farsighted projects, ones that are able to understand the historical-social future in its most crucial aspects.

V. WHICH PLURALISM?

Pluralism is a term today of great importance and full of varying meanings. If we wanted to establish its various definitions, we could state that by the term 'pluralism one attempts today to indicate the legitimacy of coexistence of divergent general conceptions of thought, at times also opposed, that come from cultures that are different from each other'.[38] Pluralism has always – and for this reason one would commit a great error if one held it to be a phenomenon exclusively of modernity – expressed itself as 'a political doctrine that seeks to confute the monolithic theory of the State', becoming, then, 'equally an analysis of human societies and institutions different from the State'.[39] If anything, modernity has had a different approach to the problem and has generated some 'techniques' that are able to assess it and also, in certain cases, to 'measure it'.

From what has been observed hitherto, it emerges that the genesis and the meanings of pluralism are somewhat ancient. Confining ourselves to the contemporary epoch, we should affirm that one of the first great theoreticians was Montesquieu who had the courage to propose anew the division of powers and the role of the intermediate bodies against the trend towards the concentration and unification

---

38 I summarise here the heading of S. Caramella and A. Giuliani, 'Pluralismo', in *Enciclopedia filosofica* (Lucarini, su licenza della Casa Editrice Le Lettere, Florence, 1982), vol. VI, pp. 641ff.

39 *Ibid.*, p. 645.

of power typical of the formation of the modern State.[40] An attempt was made, in other words, to remove from a State that was held to be all-powerful, religion, the economy and more in general part of what was held to be the domain of the sphere of the State.

At the outset, even if not contemporaneously, pluralism had two different political approaches: liberalism and democratic theory. Only after some time to this was added the socialist outlook. It was, however, above all else liberalism that strengthened pluralism as the possibility of creating different centres of power. All of this was to dismantle the approach of the absolutist State and generate new and different ideas of the State.

It is clear that in introducing the criterion of the pluralistic State one would end up by calling into question the State understood as the sole source of authority. At this point, there would have been the possibility of assessing other sources of authority that were present, albeit with a different importance and influence, in the life of society. Subsequently there were many critical positions of a Christian outlook that did not confine themselves to criticising the State, which was seen as the enemy of pluralism, but also broadened their criticism to liberal ideas which were seen as overly individualistic and thus no less dangerous. Statism and individualism were thus understood as two different sides of the same coin, sides that would tend to eliminate the social formations that occupy intermediate spaces.[41] It follows from this that

---

40 Cf. on this point N. Bobbio, *Teoria generale della politica* (Giulio Einaudi Editore, Turin, 1999), pp. 271ff. On Montesquieu's thought on this subject see the second part of chap. IV in R. Pezzimenti, *The Open Society along the Arduous Path of Modernity, with Letters from Isaiah Berlin and Hilary Putnam* (Gracewing Fowler Wright Books, Leominster, 2011).

41 Cf. M. Serio, *Il mito della democrazia sociale. Giovanni Gronchi e la cultura politica dei cattolici italiani (1902-1955)* (Rubbettino, Soneria

pluralism seen from a perspective permeated by religiosity had to seem different to liberal pluralism understood in a secular sense.

One now understands why despite accusations that have not always been sound, Christian social thought has always been 'pluralistic' because it has postulated the mediation between the individual and the State of certain intermediate bodies such as the family, local communities with their own local government, professional organisations, natural and spontaneous aggregations, and yet others. It was from this perspective that the debate about the *way of conceiving political unity itself was born*. Faced with a monolithic unity of a clear Platonic impress, the criterion appeared of 'harmonious unity' which contemplated the logic of differences that were nonetheless capable of pursuing 'shared ends'. These two different approaches gradually became clarified and found their roots in a different way of understanding human beings in their contexts. This harmonious unity no longer conceived man as a political animal but as a social animal and, as such, able to belong to various forms of aggregation.

Such forms are provided by intermediate bodies. The *anti-pluralist theories* of some modern States, which do not accept citizens that are capable of pursuing different interests and thus of belonging to various social groups that are even in contrast with each other, have opposed these bodies. Thus it was that pluralism appeared as a *moment of mediation* between the State and the individual for whose salvation not even grandiose reflections on the state of nature were enough. Indeed, it should be remembered that not all the theories of nature, despite their propositions, were favourable to intermediate bodies and to pluralism.

Mannelli, 2000), p. 6.

Only some political approaches were favourable to a plural society. Amongst these, the pluralism typical of the socialist approach was the one that we may define as functional. Certainly if we think of Marxist socialism, all of this appears not very likely, but one should realise that the first and fiercest critic of Marxism was himself a socialist – Proudhon. This French thinker engaged in a radical overturning of the traditional relationship between civil society and the State. Acting from an approach that referred to the emphasis on associations of Fourier and Saint-Simon, he supported a multiplicity of social groupings to which each individual relates according to his or her own aptitudes and needs. It is no accident that Proudhon looked to families and then to workers' companies, kinds of anonymous societies whose shares workers owned and were called upon to manage.[42] All of this, after a certain fashion, invoked centralisation, could be defined as anti-pluralistic, and Marxism itself was its most extreme expression. Indeed, Proudhon wanted to create a perfect society[43] in which there would no longer be room for political criticism. Proudhon prefigured that *conflict-ridden pluralism based upon rules* that would be specific to contemporary democracy and which, with suitable adjustments, would be implemented with the British Labour Party. Here the most genuine proposals of socialism would seek to conjoin with those of trade unionism. The need would arise to create a sort of *ethics of conflict*, of confrontation, that is to say, based upon rules and not upon clashes in the street that would lead to revolutionary ideals.

---

42 R. Pezzimenti, *The Open Society along the Arduous Path of Modernity, with Letters from Isaiah Berlin and Hilary Putnam*, 10.12.

43 On this subject the thoughts of Rosmini are illuminating but here I would like to refer to what by now is a classic of political science, above all some chapters of the first part of G. Sartori, *Democrazia e definizioni* (Il Mulino, Bologna, 1972).

This idea was also advanced by Christian thinkers such as Maritain and Mounier. Reference was thus made to a pluralist State that moved from the Labour vision to that of the 'social-Christians' who *completely accepted the democratic outlook*. For these authors, the greater the possibility of forming associations the greater the bulwark against the possible tyranny of the majority, which was a further danger for the life of pluralism. The freedom to form associations was *the freedom of minorities* and their capacity to keep pluralism alive. Associations, indeed, would not have needed to exist if they had to represent the interests of the majority. We here have an example that bears witness to how extreme democracy prevents the very dangers of democracy.[44]

This certainly positive aspect, however, had a negative consequence – that of an expansion in the number of possible participants that does not always bring to the fore the most admirable personalities. Eminent men distance themselves from political life so as not to be the victims of too many compromises.[45] Whatever the case, it is precisely the interest of the majority of people in the affairs of social life that ended up by circumscribing and not increasing the tasks of the central power. This emphasis on associations therefore meant the *mutual limitation of sovereignty*, an authentic guarantee of pluralism. It should be observed, however, that the people, as well, *cannot be the only* legitimate sovereign because the people, too, can become an absolute sovereign.

If in concrete terms *pluralism highlights an expression of interests as well*, the need arises to give rise to structures that certain interests know how to channel. From associations one thus moves on to groups and then to parties. The aim is

---

44 Cf. A. de Tocqueville, *Democracy in America*, pp. 224-226.
45 Cf. *Ibid.*, pp. 229-232.

to give interests channels and means of access not only for their organisation or aggregation but also for their success. [46]

In America membership of a group seems to matter more than membership of a class as is the case in Europe. This also derives from that religious consciousness, typical of the American people, that increases the need – above all at a local level – to take on responsibilities. This sort of social Christianity developed only a little later in the old continent.

Social Christianity, whatever the case, exercised great influence, above all in the middle of the twentieth century, even though it had roots that were already evident a century prior to that. It tried to balance two different positions that were then dominant: establishing itself as the 'holder of the balance of power', on the one hand, as has already been observed, between statism and individualism understood as being responsible for the problems of modernity, and highlighting, on the other, that *freedom and property* could not be understood as ends in themselves but as *instrumental goods* directed towards achieving the common good and the good of the person.[47] At the end of the nineteenth century and the beginning of the twentieth century there was already a great deal of Catholic thought about pluralism. In Italy much of this flowed into the formation of the ideals of the People's Party.

On 18 January 1919 Don Sturzo, in what can be called the 'Manifesto of the People's Party', explicitly affirmed that the State *had to respect* various natural organisms such

---

[46] Amongst the very many studies that have addressed this subject I would like to refer to one, perhaps a little dated but by now a classic: G.A. Almond, G. Bingham Powell Jnr. and G. Pasquino (eds.) *Politica comparata* (Il Mulino, Bologna, 1970). To refer to another classic text see the section 'Partiti politici e gruppi di pressione', in G. Sartori (ed.), *Antologia di Scienza politica* (Il Mulino, Bologna, 1970).

[47] Cf. M. Serio, *Il mito della democrazia sociale*, p. 6.

as the family, social classes, local communities with their own local government etc. He thus ended up by arguing in favour of a society understood as a 'plural' organism. In the 'Constitution of the Party', it is possible to encounter all the terms of the pluralism of Sturzo. In addition to subjects relating to the family, explicit reference is made to: 'freedom of teaching at every level...Legal recognition and freedom of class organisation in trade union unity... The freedom and autonomy of local public agencies, associations and authorities...Reorganisation of charity and public aid towards forms of welfare. Respect for the freedom of private initiatives and institutions...The freedom and independence of the Church in the full performance of its spiritual magisterium...Freedom of, and respect for, the Christian conscience...General and local taxation reform'.[48] Amongst the other points, there stands out that relating to electoral reform which, as regards pluralism, envisaged an 'elected Senate with a prevalent representation of the bodies of the nation (academic bodies, local government, provincial government, organised classes').[49]

Pluralism thus acquired one of its fundamental contents: that of opposing the pantheistic State. In line with the whole of a tradition, Sturzo was able to affirm: 'To the State is attributed a pre-eminent function over the whole of society, because to the State is attributed *power*, *law* and *force*. Here as well one should bear in mind that power, law and force are by innate need the characteristics of every social form, albeit within the limits of its own aims and according to different historical implementations'.[50] Sturzo therefore

---

48 L. Sturzo, *Il partito popolare italiano (1919-1922)*, vol. I (Nicola Zanichelli Editore, Bologna, 1956), pp. 69ff.

49 *Ibid.*, p. 71.

50 L. Sturzo, *La società. Sua natura e leggi. Sociologia Storicistica* (Nicola Zanichelli Editore, Bologna, 1949), p. 67.

also prescribed to the State, which he wrote with a capital letter, limitations. Otherwise there would disappear even the existence of the other social forms and pluralism itself.

It was the champions of Christian pluralism who exercised a decisive influence in the composition of article 2 of the Italian Constitution: 'The Republic recognises and guarantees the inviolable rights of the person, as an individual and in the social groups where human personality is expressed. The Republic expects that the fundamental duties of political, economic and social solidarity be fulfilled'. There were even some, like the deputy Marchesi, who wanted an even more explicit exposition and suggested for this article a reference to 'interior freedom, which cannot be given or removed by any government...the supreme goal of the personal destiny of the individual, cannot be regulated or imperilled by the law'.[51]

However, specifically in upholding pluralism, understood as a value that had been denied by authoritarian regimes, in the West the first criticisms began to be made, not to mention in some cases examples of opposition to pluralism itself. We can say that it was perceived as a sort of loss due to the fact, as Huntington argues, that the 'move from a traditional society to a modern society was more dramatic in the field of political beliefs and ideologies'.[52] This is why, above all else in the United States of America, pluralism was at the outset accused at a theoretical level and held to be guilty of providing a distorted picture of American society. Even more relevant was the criticism made of pluralism at an

---

51 V. Falzone, F. Palermo and F. Cosentino (eds.), *La Costituzione della Repubblica italiana illustrata con i lavori preparatori* (Mondadori Editore, Milan, 1976), p. 28.

52 S. P. Huntingdon, 'La politica nella società post-industriale', in G. Urbani (ed.), *Sindacati e politica nella società post-industriale*, *Quaderni della Rivista italiana di Scienza politica* (Il Mulino, Bologna, 1976), p. 158.

ideological level. In the view of some critics, it had not been realised that 'every social group has a natural tendency to a rigidity of its structures as the number of its members grows and the range of its activities is extended. An apparently pluralistic society is in reality polycratic, that is to say it has a number of centres of power, where each one makes its own claims prevail over the claims of its members'.[53] Thinkers such as C. Wright Mills and H. Marcuse voiced this criticism.

The former in his famous text expressed furious criticisms of some groups who, after following a fruitful pathway of coexistence, had occupied the vital settings of American politics.[54] They had ended up by deciding for the overwhelming majority of Americans, who were by now forced to live a stereotypical life that was deprived of any original stimulus. To sum up, in spite of pluralism, the albeit advanced American democracy had acquired a totalitarian model, although one camouflaged by democratic methods. The criticism levelled by Marcuse was more critical. In his *One-dimensional Man*, this philosopher of German origins sought to react to what he believed was a new form of totalitarianism – technological rationality. *'That which is cannot be true.* To our well-trained ears this statement appears frivolous and ridiculous, or scandalous like the other that seems to say the opposite: *what is real is rational'*.[55] The return to Hegel (Marx should be reappraised in terms of this aspect of Hegel's thought) restored to pluralism a neo-

---

[53] N. Bobbio, 'Pluralismo', in N. Bobbio, N, Matteucci and G. Pasquino, (eds.), *Dizionario di politica*, p. 722.

[54] Cf. C. Wright Mills *The Power Elite* (Oxford University Press, New York, 1956).

[55] H. Marcuse, *One-dimensional Man. Studies in the Ideology of Advanced Industrial Society* (Beacon Press, Boston, 1968), p. 123.

idealist impress and generated the danger of a return to an abstract pluralism.

This reference to Hegel led to a historicising of the question of pluralism. For many this was a call to concreteness, above all if freed from the abstruseness of dialectics. Truly interesting observations emerged from this, even if they were not completely new. In the view of some, indeed, pluralism had to be read in relation to a set of goods that 'have a history of transactions, not only between them but also in relation to the material and moral world in which they exist',[56] which means that a single measurement of judgement does not exist and cannot exist. This belief opened up pluralism to the risk of relativism or the syncretism of values with a consequent 'trivialisation' of pluralism itself, *generating thereby the irrelevance of values*. To obviate this difficulty, it even came to be argued 'that a theory of justice cannot be achieved without pre-supposing a given and stable map of social practices involving the construction and sharing of meanings'.[57] This is true but insufficient, because this approach, which confers on pluralism only a historical value, also deprives it of any possible universal recognition.

One should engage in a clarification about pluralism which only Christian pluralism with its concreteness appears able to do. Indeed, as much as this may be obvious, one is dealing with reformulating pluralism itself and this runs the risk of becoming formal or, even worse, abstract. Pluralism is abstract when it is presented only as formal respect for ideas. In reality, at times, many of these ideas can be blamed, but what matters is respect for the individuals who are their bearers. Otherwise in many cases one ends up by speaking a great deal about pluralism, with words, and at

---

56   M. Walzer, *Sfere di giustizia* (Feltrinelli, Milan, 1987), p. 19.

57   S. Veca, *La filosofia politica* (Laterza, Bari-Rome, 2005), p. 91.

the same time sending dissent to the gulag or concentration camps. True pluralism, on the other hand, is the pluralism that allows me not to share, and even to combat, certain ideas, such as, for example, the death penalty, but obliges me to respect those who are the bearers of those ideas.

This applies above all else today, in a multi-ethnic and multicultural society, 'in order to achieve a coexistence that tends towards harmony, an interaction',[58] and which is possible only if we base it on the inalienable premise of the person and his or her rights.

---

[58] P. Malizia, *Al plurale. Declinazioni di una società multietnica e multiculturale* (Franco Angeli, Milan, 2008), p. 11.

VI. EDUCATING PEOPLE IN POLITICAL AND SOCIAL REPRESENTATION

The debate about the ends of politics is not topical and is scarcely evident in the principal contemporary philosophical interpretations. It has been replaced by abundant analyses of the instruments, procedures and rules needed to produce political decisions. We are truly far away in time from the Greek world when, in asking what the purpose of politics was, it was argued that politics had the purpose of achieving happiness, or, in the Roman world, justice. Today we are much less ambitious. But even we ourselves cannot escape the basic question, otherwise why should we be interested in politics? It is certainly no accident that many people, perhaps too many people, today are losing interest in politics.

1. 'Excess of democracy'

More than one philosopher of politics, like some political scientists, have posed to themselves the problem of outlining the so-called 'minimum benefits of politics'.[59] 'Minimum' – that is to say really achievable to avoid the creation of disappointments with a consequent lack of interest in politics. This is the great political problem of our times, what Rosanvallon defines as the 'érosion *de la confiance*

---

[59] B. Crick, *In Defence of Politics* (Penguin, London, 1962); Italian edition: *Difesa della Politica* (Il Mulino, Bologna, 1969), p. 7.

des citoyens dans leurs dirigeants'.[60] The real problem is that this erosion seems to be destined to increase rather than decrease. It may appear a paradox, but this sickness that is afflicting developed democracies – and they have been like this for a long time – appears to be the outcome of a purported 'excess of democracy'. Obviously, this is a paradox typical of those political systems in which 'an overload of questions compared to the possibilities of answers of institutions'[61] has been generated. Can this exaggeration be overcome? What role can political education play in the overcoming of this paradox? To begin with, perhaps, it would be appropriate to ask if this lack of trust in politics is not a consequence of that spreading scepticism that emerges in the dominant culture of a world that sees itself as being more evolved. If this were the case, politics would be nothing else but one of the expressions of the pessimism and the lack of objectives that more in general, today, marks existence.

This would also explain why, although speaking generically about anti-politics, it is very difficult to reach a 'univocal definition'. As always occurs, it is precisely the lack of this univocal element that has brought about the growing acceptance of the term 'in the rhetoric used by political actors themselves'.[62] This rhetoric, in my view, is the litmus test of a phenomenon that is rather evident and attests, on the part of the citizens, to the end of an illusion: that of being able really to count in the domain of political decisions.

---

60 P. Rosanvallon, *La contre-democratie. La politique à l'âge de la défiance* (Éd. Du Seuil, Paris, 2006), p. 9.

61 M. Truffelli, 'Autorità versus libertà. Il pensiero antipolitico nelle democrazie contemporanee', in Nicola Antonetti (ed.) *Libertà e autorità nelle democrazie contemporanee. Percosi di ricerca* (Rubbettino Editore, Soveria Mannelli, 2008), p. 193.

62 *Ibid.*, p. 196.

To understand matters correctly, the end of this illusion has precise roots and it is also the not always conscious outcome of those totalitarian and statist visions that dominated the political culture of the twentieth century, a culture that 'highlighted the inadequacy of the responses that...politics, despite everything being centred around the state dimension, was able to provide'. This incapacity of politics is highlighted by the 'implosion of the form of the political party and the difficulties encountered by all representative systems'.[63]. The crisis of the state dimension is not, however, the only reason for disenchantment with politics. Another reason can be perceived in the move from modernity to post-modernity, to the age of uncertainty and resentment, and to the decline of political engagement. All of these are symptoms of that liquid modernity[64] which is a synonym for a lack of certain points of reference and, as I will observe below, also of the obscuring of that *sense of limits* typical of political culture until the threshold of the twentieth century.

2. The fracture between society and politics and the implosion of the latter

It has been rightly said that 'power (namely the ability to do) has been separated from politics (namely the ability to decide what to do and with which priority)' but I would add that politics has, in its turn, been separated from society. Hence, as Bauman says, the frailty, the provisional character and the vulnerability that characterise our days, which we are experiencing in an increasingly hurried way, without the ability to find anchorages. Hence, even more, 'the increasingly strong conviction that the *only* constant is

---

63 *Ibid.*, pp. 200, 197.
64 Cf. *ibid.*, p. 198.

change and the *only* certainty is uncertainty'.⁶⁵ This is also the consequence of those philosophies that have subscribed to the idea of the perfect society since the nineteenth century.

The criticisms made of Bernstein by a Left founded upon conceptions of a future static perfection are a demonstration of this. The uncertainty in which we live is the outcome of a complicated combination to which the crisis of an idea of Enlightenment freedom, feelings of ignorance and powerlessness in finding solutions, as well as other factors, contribute.⁶⁶ To attribute 'value to the future'⁶⁷ seems to have become the objective of a society that has lost its way. Rosmini would say that we are again obliged to address the question of happiness which can certainly not depend only on the search for profit.

Unravelled societies are poor in ties and thus in stability. Those few ties that do resist appear to critics to be outside current reality and without meaning. To this is added what can be seen as the problem of our times: 'power has become quintessentially *extra-territorial*'.⁶⁸ The absence of power means the impossibility of controlling it. The absence of rules, 'or mere unclarity of norms – anomie – is the worst lot which may occur to people as they struggle to cope with their life-tasks'.⁶⁹ Is it still meaningful to

---

65 Z. Bauman, *Liquid Modernity* (Polity Press, Cambridge, UK – Malden, MA, USA, 2006); Italian edition: *Modernità liquida* (Editori Laterza, Bari-Rome, 2011), pp. VI-VII. For the quotations referring to Roman numerals the reference is to the 'Prefazione' written for the Italian edition *La modernità liquida rivisitata*. For the other quotations the reference is to the edition in English.

66 Cf. *ibid.*, pp. XI-XIII.

67 *Ibid.*, p. XIX.

68 *Ibid.*, p. XXXIII.

69 Z. Bauman, *Liquid Modernity*, pp. 20-21.

speak about representation and, as its consequence, about responsibility? To say, as some have argued, amongst them Alain Touraine, that the sociality of man is over seems to me to be too reductive. 'What is wrong in the society we live in, said Cornelius Castoriadis, is that it stopped questioning itself'.[70] Yet it is equally certain that we have to start from the retrieval of social participation without which there can be no civil life. Few people seem to realise how the cardinal elements of our democracies have been reduced. The propensity to oppose seems to have disappeared, perhaps because, as Havel said, 'opposition is precisely every attempt to live in truth'[71] and this seems to have disappeared from post-modern culture.

The century of the totalitarian dimension was the century of the reduction of the human being to being an *exclusively* political animal. All of this brought about a blind trust in the political dimension, which was then tragically disappointed, but it also caused a limitation and subsequent abolition of the social dimension. There followed from this a gradual reduction of freedom and therefore of participation and responsibility.

This observation, however, cannot avoid a serious question: can anti-politics really see itself as such or does it, too, constitute an illusion on a level with the pan-political vision of a totalitarian approach with its derivations of various kinds? In my view, anti-politics runs the risk of being like anti-philosophy. Taking up the ancient adage according to which in order to combat philosophy it is always necessary to engage in philosophy (some people would say renewed philosophy but it always remains philosophy), to combat politics we cannot rely on anti-

---

70 *Ibid.*, p. 22.

71 V. Havel, *Il potere dei senza potere* (La Casa di Matriona, Milan – Itaca, Castel Bolognese, 2013), p. 75.

politics[72] which always remains a version, which I believe to be dangerous, of politics *tout court*. Indeed, one may say that anti-politics is a form of political struggle, but in whose hands? This is a concern that not everyone has but which nonetheless requires adequate answers.

We should not forget that there are those who have wanted to outline precursors of anti-politics, albeit ones different from each other, in thinkers such as Hobbes and Rousseau[73] and this should make us reflect. Certainly one cannot deny that the man from Geneva thought that 'representation was a threat to democracy'.[74] In the same way, we cannot ignore that the phenomenon that has exploded today is a consequence of a lack of confidence in that parliamentary system that has constituted an arduous achievement– in the view of many a repeat achievement[75] – of modernity.

---

72 T. Mann, *Betrachtungen eines Unpolitischen* (S. Fischer Verlag, Berlin, 1918); Italian edition: *Considerazioni di un impolitico* (Adelphi, Milan, 1997), p. 418.

73 Cf. B. Crick, *In Defence of Politics*, p. 202.

74 Cf. H. Fenichel Pitkin, 'Representation and Democracy: Uneasy Alliance', in *The Concept of Representation*; Italian edition: *Il concetto di rappresentanza*, with a 'Prefazione' by A. Pizzorno (Rubbettino Editore, Soveria Mannelli, 2017), p. XXXIV. For the quotations that refer to Roman numerals the reference is to the essay in the Italian edition. For the other quotations the reference is to the edition in English: *The Concept of Representation* (University of California Press, Berkeley and Los Angeles, 1972).

75 In reality there are many studies, with which I agree, that argue that the epoch of absolutism interrupted that journey towards modern representation that unfolded through the Middle Ages, taking up some assumptions of the classical world. Of fundamental importance here was the rediscovery of Roman law on which was based the autonomy of communes and the maritime republics. Amongst many studies on this subject cf. R. Pezzimenti, *The Open Society and its Friends, with Letters from Isaiah Berlin and Karl R. Popper.*

During moments of distrust in politics there are those who seek to react by offering anew a technocratic vision. I do not want here to highlight the risks of such an approach to which, for that matter, for more or less two centuries, every so often, reference has been made. What I would like to emphasise is that this approach tends only to 'dethrone politics' and to replace it with science, technology and economics. Politics in this way becomes 'an obsolete hindrance, a rusty machine directed toward sectional interests that are superfluous and counterproductive for the general welfare',[76] as well as unable to solve practical problems.

In these ways of thinking, politics is no longer useful, it is no longer perceived as being needed. How did we reach such a perception of being a politician? We have to be honest and say that if the *Left* was responsible for offering politics in an all-embracing state dimension that then led to its implosion, the *Right* bears no less responsibility given that it aimed solely at containing such an undertaking. In the meantime, amongst the two litigants a third and not foreseen intruder prevailed: a certain type of neo-individualism that aimed only at pursuing its own selfish happiness. This approach, relegating to secondary importance discourses about the common good, inevitably reduced politics in importance.

Many intellectuals greeted this approach as a positive development given that in their view finally in Europe, too, we were witnessing a definitive affirmation of liberal thought. As far as I am concerned, this idea seems to me not only debatable but also superficial. European liberalism, with a few exceptions, has never been so exaggeratedly individualistic. One need only consider the difference,

---

[76] M. Truffelli, *Autorità* versus *libertà. Il pensiero antipolitico nelle democrazie contemporanee*, pp. 217-218.

which is not only of a terminological kind, between what we Europeans call 'liberalism' and what the Americans define as 'libertarianism'. It is certainly no accident that European liberalism in the eyes of very many American intellectuals is liberal-conservatism. The fact remains, however, that one of the current goals of politics is to redefine the boundaries between the domain specific to society and that specific to the individual. Without, however, forgetting that this last, for a great deal of European culture (above all of the Christian tradition), should be further defined in order to outline the space that belongs to the person and the space that belongs to the individual. When I say this, I am not thinking only of the personalist approach.

3. Representation and participation

Behind such observations there is the belief that despite the fact that some people rightly argue that freedom is almost a synonym for politics, there is also another approach that holds that politics cannot be reduced solely to the – albeit important – question of freedom. This last, indeed, cannot in any way be separated from other values, such as equality, justice, representation, the possibility of participation and yet others.

Some of these values are extremely interconnected. One may think of political representation which, quite apart from the difficulties of definition,[77] is an undoubted instrument of political participation, to the point of becoming an authentic 'specialised profession in the organisation of the State' and useful in channelling the requests of the electors. On the condition, however, that these are constantly engaged a) in those activities of connection that we could define as being

---

77 Cf. on this point the work, which by now is a classic, of H. Fenichel Pitkin, *The Concept of Representation*.

'extra-parliamentary', and b) do not participate solely in periodically held elections but are also vigilant and make proposals. As regards the *first point*, citizens should participate actively in movements, associations, pressure groups, demonstrations, petitions, and other realities as well; with respect to the *second*, an active role should be played, for example, in *referendums*. Overall, participation should avoid a lack of interest in political activity, which brings about 'an apparently apolitical popular presence'.[78] One should here emphasise the adverb 'apparently' because there may be citizens who, although they remain extraneous to political activity, are nonetheless able to play an important social role such as to compensate for failings in the political sphere.

This participation could also compensate for what for some people is another 'incongruence' of political representation, namely the complete 'autonomy of the elected in relation to all control by the voters'. This is an aspect which in itself is not to be looked down on if the elected were really the best 'to obtain certain positions in the service of the State'.[79] In this case, the complete independence of the elected would have a meaning.[80] In many instances such is not the case and thus people continue 'to believe that the system functions even if in reality power, like those who control it, continues to be far from citizens',[81] if not indeed against them.

---

78 Cf. A. Pizzorno, 'Prefazione' to H. Fenichel Pitkin, *Il concetto di rappresentanza*, pp. XVI-XVII.

79 Cf. *ibid.*, p. XXI.

80 On this subject see the by now classic speech of Edmund Burke to the electors of Bristol, but above all 'An Appeal from the New to the Old Whigs', in *The Works of Edmund Burke*, vol. V (The World's Classics, Oxford University Press, Oxford, 1928).

81 Cf. A. Pizzorno, 'Prefazione', p. XXIV.

The advantages of representation are usually highlighted by those who argue that liberal-democratic representation is a step forward compared to corporative representation. Yet the latent corporatism that afflicts a significant number of post-modern countries, such as Italy, is often ignored. These are forms that make control of those who are sent by those who send them impossible. From what has been said hitherto, it emerges that representation alone does not constitute a guarantee for the existence of a democracy.

Those who combat representation, even today, do so on the basis of an old prejudice raised centuries ago by those conservatives who, even when they ended up by accepting representation, 'far from equating it with democracy, used it as an instrument to prevent the democratic impulse and to control the turbulent lower classes...the prevalent result was that representation took the place of democracy instead of placing itself at its service'.[82] It is certainly no accident that Rousseau was ironical about the feeling of freedom of the English who, in his view, believed they were free only because they had the right to vote. But to return to such positions certainly does not facilitate the advance of democracy. What we need to do is to put at the side of democracy instruments that will make it effective and functional in order to avoid political life being reduced to that 'silent' consent that would certainly disappear if the world of government solely defended the privileges of the few. One of the means to avoid this danger can be actuated when at a local level citizens take part in democratic affairs in their districts, controlling the local representatives who, in their turn, then become spokesmen with national representatives.

---

82   H. Fenichel Pitkin, 'Representation and Democracy: Uneasy Alliance', pp. XXXIX-XLI.

4. Social representation as a safeguard for political representation and democratic power

In order to understand to the full what has been outlined, we should reflect on the meaning of the current term 'representation' as it emerged (or re-emerged) from its Latin meaning, transferred later to its English meaning starting in the thirteenth century. Indeed, we should remember that 'persons sent to participate in church councils or in the English parliament came gradually to be thought of as representatives'.[83] Many of these at the outset were already elected.[84] It is sufficient to think of the multiple experiences of communes, autonomous cities and maritime republics that were present in many parts of Europe. It was from the Middle Ages onwards that representatives saw themselves as such because they represented the whole nation given that the principle, which was upheld subsequently, began to gain ground that representation was necessary given that the people could not act collectively.

It would be more interesting to ask ourselves the reasons for this phenomenon and why it arose specifically during the medieval period. The reason, or one of the reasons, can be traced back to the renewed use of Roman law. How crucial this rediscovery was can be easily understood if we think that it brought about the rediscovery of representation, above all in the social sphere and only as a consequence in the political domain. The latter was seen – rightly – as being narrower, even though equally important, as the former. The same criterion, which was then expressed in England,

---

83 H. Fenichel Pitkin, *The Concept of Representation*, p. 3.

84 Fenichel Pitkin does not agree with this but he forgets that well before the granting of the *Magna Carta Libertatum* in a large part of Europe the criterion of election was in force in many communes, autonomous cities and city republics.

of the unsustainability of taxation without representation, attests to the importance of the question. Only if one forgets social representation does political representation become sustainable. In this way, one explains the pessimism of those who argue that true representation not only does not exist but can only be injurious. And this also explains the disagreement that exists amongst scholars about the question of the use of the term itself.

I believe that in relation to this question we encounter a complex cultural inheritance. From idealism onwards – and idealism alone is not to blame for this – we retrieved a pan-political vision with a Greek basis and we strongly reduced the social vision of political life typical of the Roman tradition. All of this brought about a reading anew of certain authors, classic ones as well, attributing to them an approach that they did not in the least have. One need only consider how St. Augustine was reinterpreted in a neo-Platonic way and this characterised a precise approach of Christian political thought as well. One needs to consider again how, starting with Western Patristic thought, the cultural heritage of Varro, Cicero and others was of decisive importance for moral, anthropological and social thinking. When referring to these figures, St. Augustine explicitly said: 'If these philosophers want the life of the wise man to be social, we want this even more'.[85] This was a crucial observation that looked forward to the criterion of participation. The true wise man is not he who aims only at contemplative activity but he who optimises the *appetitus ad agendum*, 'who moves towards a multiple and varied activity, from that of knowledge to public and moral activity'.[86] To know is to act on a par with other activities.

---

85 Augustine, *De Civ. Dei*, XIX, 5.

86 N. Cipriani, 'Lo schema dei tria vitia (voluptas, superbia, curiositas) nel De vera religione: Antropologia soggiacente e fonti' in *Augustinianum*, Annus XXXVIII, Fasciculus I, Iunius 1998, p. 178.

For that matter, Cicero was very clear on this point: 'we were born to act. But there are two kinds of activity... observation and knowledge...the management of public affairs is the science of this management'.[87] This seems to prefigure the position of Fichte who criticised dualism, and not only the dualism of Kant, but of all epochs – knowledge relating to knowledge is *ad agendum*. The morality that must accompany scholars in their gnoseological activity is not different from moral and public activity, not least because actions must be directed towards precise goals. That there is a link *ad agendum* is demonstrated by the fact that activities need peace and security (*tranquillitas sine difficultate*). Only in this way will it be possible to achieve the goals of various actions and this will be granted 'to those who in knowledge love only truth, in action only peace, and in the body only health'.[88]

The overcoming of dualism seems to me to be typical of Varro. It has been observed[89] in relation to him that Augustine, even though he criticised his approach of immanence, accepts his eudemonistic approach. This idea has certainly not been appreciated by traditional interpreters. The fact however remains that specifically on the basis of this eudemonology St. Augustine 'rejects the persistent concerns of Plotinus and Porphyrius about the negative consequences for the soul of its descent into the body'. And it is also from the Roman world that there comes

---

87 Cicero, *De Finibus Bonorum et Malorum* (William Heinemann LDT, London – The MacMillan Co., New York), MCMXIV, V, XXI, 58.

88 Augustine, *De vera religione*, 53, 103.

89 N. Cipriani, 'L'influsso di Varrone sul pensiero antropologico e morale nei primi scritti di S. Agostino', in AA. Vv, *L'etica cristiana nei secoli III e IV: Eredità e confronti*, XXIV *Incontro di studiosi dell'antichità cristiana*, Roma, 4-6 maggio 1995 (Institutum Patristicum Augustinianum, Rome, 1996), p. 374.

that 'anthropological and moral approach that, compared to neo-Platonism, emphasises much more...the values of the body and social life'.[90] This is the outcome of the action of associates and does not belong to the political sphere.

In his *De Ordine*, 'Augustine makes clear that man is superior to animals not so much because he does ordered things, of which animals are also capable, but because he knows the laws of order',[91] and, one could add, the aims of his actions. This is a position typical of Cicero that describes *societas* as a set of individuals, partners, who aim at a shared goal, observing shared rules: *ubi societas ibi ius*. These rules are dictated by the partners and not by politics. It is deduced from this that a human being could even pass his existence distant from political engagement but not from social engagement given that is it in this domain that he expresses his nature, and his morality as well. This last, indeed, is the specific outcome of the society from which the subject emerges. This is a living tradition and it is susceptible, through further participation, to further and ongoing deepening and adjustment.

Associates have the obligation to keep the peace in the coexistence of civil society in order to enjoy all those goods that, without rules and without peace, would run the risk of being lost. It is precisely this agreement between rules that govern various societies that generates for Cicero that *consensus iuris* that makes 'stable the concord of citizens in commanding and obeying, creating in them a certain agreement of will as regards the pertinent goods of this mortal life'.[92] In addition to these general goods, there are the specific goods of the body – an idea again taken from Varo – that form an authentic hierarchy. Some of these,

---

90 *Ibid.*, pp. 388, 396.
91 *Ibid.*, p. 380.
92 Augustine, *De Civ. Dei*, XIX, 17.

such as beauty and physical strength, are not in the least 'indispensable in the acquiring of virtue'. To these one can add others, such as 'the agility of members and corporeal pleasure itself [which] can be looked for licitly not for their own sake but solely with a view to others (health and the integrity of the senses and the members and first of all life)'.[93] In this outlook, the young Augustine saw even pleasure of the senses as a good of the body,[94] which could be seen as an expression of a certain morality.

Today to defend the role of social man is no longer only, as was once said, to defend the intermediary bodies and civil society. It is self-evident that this is taken for granted, but there is something more that is new. Today we no longer have to defend ourselves against a power – as could have been the case in the past – that is invasive and oppressive. Today we have to give back a political role to a power that no longer exists. There are rightly those who state that today 'power…sails away from the street and the market-place, from assembly halls and parliaments, local and national governments, and beyond the reach of citizens control, into the extraterritoriality of electronic networks'[95] or to other domains that are even more inaccessible. The power, the power that is of use, an expression of representation, is today as needed as ever before to defend our freedom.

---

93 N. Cipriani, 'Augustine, *De Civ. Dei*, XIX, p. 17. L'influsso di Varrone sul pensiero antropologico e morale nei primi scritti di S. Agostino', pp. 397-398.

94 Although it is not one of the most important, the *voluptas corporis*, although always a natural good 'is useful and inseparable from certain actions of the senses, indispensable for the preservation of life, like eating, drinking and procreating'. As regards 'the necessities of life, the perception of pleasure is not at all irrational or illicit'. The important thing is to distinguish what is useful from what is harmful because the latter cannot make man happy but only deceive him: *ibid.*, p. 398.

95 Z. Bauman, *Liquid Modernity*, p. 40.

This is obviously a power of guarantees that recognises its own limits, a power in which the modern generations, through participation, should be educated. We are living a great paradox expressed in summarising form by Bauman: 'Any true liberation calls today for more, not less, of the *public sphere* and *public power*'.[96] This is a *statement that* at first sight *could shock us* but one that can be understood only if one considers that today, given that there are too many powers 'elsewhere' and distant from citizens, the need, instead, is felt for a power that is present, produced by the will of the citizens and able to meet their needs. One of the reasons for the crisis of the very idea of Europe can be traced specifically to this distance. Not to accept this challenge is to resign oneself to the defeat of politics.

5. Representation and responsibility: the delegating of authority

In the light of what has been said, I cannot agree with the position of 'reductionist realism' which holds that 'representation exists if and only if people believe in it'.[97] One is not dealing with believing in representation but exercising it every day in common life and above all in the social domains in which we exercise our existence. No less reductive are the formalistic visions of representation. This outlook 'is shaped by the initial giving of authority, within which the representative can do whatever he pleases... There can be no such thing as representing well or badly; either he represents or he does not'.[98] This position, and the point is obvious, is a position that does not take into account the criterion of responsibility to which every office-holder

---

96 *Ibid.*, p. 51.

97 H. Fenichel Pitkin, *The Concept of Representation*, p. 9.

98 *Ibid.*, p. 39.

should be subjected. Without the criterion of responsibility, how can one assure that the person who is responsible, at least at the next electoral round, can answer for what he has done? And how can one obtain that this is separated from an assessment of whether he has managed well or badly his function as a representative?

The 'granting of authority' is another of the great questions of representation. Representative democracy is based upon the consensus of the electorate who are not systematically guided by rational choices. These observations, which to tell the truth were already being advanced more than a hundred years ago by Pareto, have been taken up by various thinkers such as, for example, Jason Brennan. His attack on representative democracy is rather simple – such democracy is not meritocratic. Whereas the power that exists in various political, economic and administrative organisms is placed in the hands of the competent, the same does not occur in the case of legislative power which in democracies is representative to the utmost. Why should it be that to fill various roles there is a need for a verification of competence but in representative politics such is not the case?

In his *Against Democracy*, Brennan seeks to offer the *epistocratic* alternative in order to correct the very many errors due to a shallow participation in political affairs. In his view, political participation corrupts and generates a decline in democracy. This is due to the fact that those who choose think only of power, that is to say of *kratos*, and do not consider the *episteme*: in substantial terms – competence. Brennan argues that the electors can be divided into three categories: the *hobbits*, the *hooligans* and the *volcanic*. The *first* have very little interest in politics and also understand it very little; the *second* know more about it but like football fans are without objectivity and are unable to assess the information that they receive; only the *third* have a good knowledge of politics and are endowed with refined reasoning, but they are very few in number.[99] Why should the ignorance and factionalism of the first two groups prevail over those who are in fact up to judging?

There is no point in observing that this analysis does not appear to be very new. I have just referred to Pareto but one could go back to Comte and if we wanted we could even go back to the philosophical rulers of Plato. The perils of such a position are in front of all of us, without taking into account that an epistocratic representation, however good it may be, would increase the detachment of the components of society in a very profound way. The errors of representation should be corrected by seeking to make representation as qualified as possible, namely through *education in democratic responsibility*. Without taking into account that giving a different weight to a vote according to the knowledge of an elector could leave to serious errors. Can culture, as Brennan argues, be the only criterion by which to establish the different weight of votes? Could not another criterion be responsibility towards those who depend on us and cannot vote, for example our children who are minors?

The question of the 'granting of authority' raises further problems. Representatives should be 'authorized in advance to act conjointly on behalf of their constituents and bind them by their collective decisions'.[100] If such is the case, how can responsibility not exist in taking decisions that

---

99 J. Brennan, *Against Democracy* (Princeton University Press, Princeton, New Jersey, 2016). This tri-partition of the electoral body is examined above all in chaps. I and II. The third deals with the corruption that takes place with political participation.

100 H. Fenichel Pitkin, *The Concept of Representation*, p. 43. In reality the quotation is taken from K. Loewenstein, *Political Power and the Governmental Process* (University of Chicago Press, Chicago, 1957), p. 38.

bind the electors? It is certainly no accident that subsequent elections have the purpose of reconsidering the previous 'granting of authority' in order to consider the advisability of entrusting authority again to the same representatives. For this reason, elections should be periodic and cannot be left to the independent decision of anybody.

Elections – as has already been observed – cannot, however, be the only element of participation in democratic life, otherwise it would be meaningless to speak about 'participatory democracy'. Without this participation, linked to a sense of responsibility, politics, and that includes democratic politics, would slide into conformism, as indeed Tocqueville reminded us. This is a position where 'accommodations are made' and which separates people from concerns about, and the shouldering of, responsibility.[101]

The problem grows worse if one thinks that it is not always possible for representatives to be the expression of a participatory democracy. 'How is it possible to proceed in all those circumstances and occasions, which are certainly not infrequent, in which in a deliberating supranational college on a *democratic* basis...there take part *representatives* of countries and peoples ruled by authoritarian, oppressive or openly criminal regimes, who are designated by those States?' The problem is a serious one but 'here we are faced with a condition of the factual acceptance of a function'.[102] The decisions taken by a supernatural organism can, in part, moderate and control the authoritarian claims of individual representatives.

---

101 Cf. G. Buttà, 'Introduzione' to F. M. Di Sciullo (ed.), *La rappresentanza nel pensiero politico nordamericano*, in *Res Publica. Rivista di studi storico-politici internazionali*, n. 18, 2017 (Rubbettino Editore, Soveria Mannelli), p. 11.

102 F.M. Di Sciullo, 'Rinascita, trasformazione o crisi della rappresentanza? Una discussione aperta', in *La rappresentanza nel pensiero politico nordamericano*, pp. 141-142.

Again citing Hanna Pitkin, one must address the problem by bearing in mind that 'the nature of representation is systemic', that is to say 'it is inseparable from the two questions of legitimacy and sovereignty'.[103] It is certainly the case that we need a qualified public opinion that is able to act 'as an *agent of selection*'. In this case, a representative is chosen as an expression 'of a group qualified in that sense'. Behind these statements lies the old problem of politics expressed by Edmund Burke and taken up by Pitkin herself who 'defined a representative through a triple relationship: with his electorate, with his party and with information'.[104] But here one would open the problem of the crisis of parties and this would deserve separate study, even if we cannot exempt it from consideration: given the troubled history of the idea of the party, its crisis could also mean a crisis of representative democracy.

Representation, to be based upon the principle of responsibility, needs suitable mechanisms of control that function better where there exists an effective division of powers and it should be observed that the traditional tripartition, theorised by Polybius and on to Montesquieu, today appears certainly insufficient. The three classic powers should be flanked by powers that have gradually become established during modernity so that in addition to the weight that they exercise we have precise rules and roles in order to avoid that they, too, going beyond their limits, come to occupy spaces that belong to other powers.

---

103 *Ibid.*, p. 141.
104 *Ibid.*, pp. 143ff.

VII. TOWARDS A NEW DIVISION OF POWERS

To begin we will start with one of the very many definitions of power: power 'is such only when it is able to condition, modify, direct, enrich and transform individual and collective lives. When, in practice, society would be profoundly different without it'.[105] It is beyond doubt, therefore, that today every discourse relating to power becomes much more complex that in the past given that we cannot be satisfied with that classic tripartition of powers which from the Roman Republic onwards animated discourse concerning what was defined as 'mixed government'. Indeed, there are more powers – many even well 'camouflaged' – that weigh upon the political order than it is possible to suppose and they orientate it in certain specific directions that do not always have a real consensus. The current political order must, therefore, reconsider the classic powers in order to make them respond to contemporary needs but it must also balance them with other powers that have formed, and which, enjoying almost an immunity, do not respect the fundamental criterion of the division of powers.

In this light it is certainly no accident that more than one voice argues that the State 'on the one hand has traditional powers designed to defend and protect individuals, and on the other hand has new powers, designed to direct the

---

[105] E. Narduzzi, *Sesto potere. Chi governa la società nell'era della tecnologia di massa e dell'innovazione permanente* (Rubbettino Editore, Soveria Mannelli, 2004), p. 3.

private activity of individuals themselves. But the crisis of the State is due to a lack of these new powers'.[106] This means that from some points of view the crisis of the liberal State and from very many angles of the democratic State, a subject that has been talked about for decades, has been more discussed than addressed. As a demonstration of this one need only think of the crisis of the legislative power.

1. The tri-partition of the classic powers and new needs

Like so many other terms of contemporary politics, 'parliament' is a term that places us 'in front of an equally disconcerting variety of forms of parliamentary forms...its substance is shown from case to case to be very varied'.[107] At its basis, and albeit with diversifications, there remain, nonetheless, certain common principles such as being 'representative', able to express the 'popular will' or 'egalitarian' – able, that is to say, to place on the same level all the participants of the assembly.

Today however, one clearly sees other needs, not least (even though this may seem paradoxical) the need for the *desiderata* of the people to become, in real terms, operational realities and not completely ignored. This has often happened in Italy, and not only in Italy,[108] for example because of the lack of the implementation of the outcome of a number of *referendums*. This highlights a certain state

---

106 P. L. Zampetti, *La democrazia partecipativa e il rinnovamento delle istituzioni* (ECIG, Genoa, 1995), p. 41. Amongst many, cf. above all A. Panebianco, *Il potere, lo stato, la libertà. La gracile costituzione della società libera* (Il Mulino, Bologna, 2004); M. Troper, *Le nuove separazioni dei poteri* (Editoriale Scientifica, Rome, 2007).

107 M. Cotta, 'Parlamento', in N. Bobbio, N. Matteucci ad G. Pasquino (eds.), *Dizionario di politica*, p. 696.

108 Cf. on this point B. Ackerman, 'The New Separation of Power', *Harvard Law Review*, volume 113, January 2000, number 3.

of intolerance within modern democracies, demonstrating how the popular will does not manage to express itself completely through traditional channels such as parties or instruments of a plebiscitary character. The state of malaise of parties is clearly highlighted by some of their most farsighted exponents who feel the need to separate themselves from the logic of apparatuses in order to draw near to the real needs for representation expressed by the people. Primaries constitute an example, certainly not of a sufficient kind, of all of this.

We may clarify immediately that to criticise some aspects of the parliamentary system does not mean 'criticism of representative democracy', just as 'not every criticism of representative democracy leads straight as a line to direct democracy'.[109]

Representative democracy has had two great merits: that of making the relations between electors and elected clear and that of allowing the various components of society an opportunity to be represented where the most important political decisions are taken. With time, however, things have become more complicated. Such a clear power ended up by giving space to a sort of invisible power. There has been an advance of what Habermas defined as the gradual emergence of the 'private sphere of the public'. All of this has brought about a series of more or less invisible powers which, however, do not answer for 'promises not kept' and, furthermore, run the risk of appearing as powers that cannot be overcome,[110] and not even — as would appear more appropriate — limited.

---

109 N. Bobbio, *Il futuro della democrazia. Una difesa delle regole del gioco* (Giulio Einaudi Editore, Turin, 1984), p. 33.

110 Cf. *ibid.*, pp. 80-81, 93. The text to which Bobbio refers is: J. Habermas, *Strukturwandel der Öffentlichkeit. Untersuchungen zu einer Kategorie der bürgerlichen Gesellschaft* (Neuwied, Berlin, 1962).

To give visibility to certain forces and to return them to the parliamentary river-bed is not always easy. Often this is not advisable given that the remedy that is proposed by some people would end up by offering anew a corporative vision, one capable, that is to say, of representing consolidated and diversified interests that clash with the most elementary canons of democracy. We should not forget, for that matter, that when we speak about groups 'the State has the task of meeting the needs of individual groups, bearing in mind, however, the needs of all the other groups'.[111] It should be observed, however, that when 'certain groups' enter parties one has to avoid them acquiring that complete 'group autonomy' that has been defined as 'groupocracy' which, more than looking for a synthesis between parties and institutions, aims solely at the pursuit of certain interests, often even ignoring those that are most urgent. If it is true, to use terminology dear to Duverger,[112] that doctrinaire parties have been replaced by those of a practical orientation and that from a society which saw the opposition of classes we have moved to a society that sees the opposition of groups, it is also true that in order to restore to parliament the role that belongs to it we have to renew it.

But all of this is not enough. The challenge, if we want to understand things as they are, is another: to lead parliament back to its true function which, together with its legislative function, is the function of control. Now there is no doubt that today some democracies have 'ended up by transforming parliament into an organ of control without power', leaving real power to the executive *alone*. 'Moreover, most of the

---

[111] P. L. Zampetti, *La democrazia partecipativa e il rinnovamento delle istituzioni*, p. 28.

[112] Cf. M. Duverger, *Les partis politiques* (Librairie Armand Colin, Paris, 1967); Italian edition: *I partiti politici*, translated by M. Cambieri Tosi (Edizioni Comunità, Milan, 1970), pp. 16ff.

laws passed are initiatives of the government and not of parliament'. And this without taking into account that in the formation of a government, as with its crisis, 'parliament is placed in front of a *fait accompli*'.[113]

In this light, perhaps it is the very criterion of representation that we should re-examine. The people cannot be understood exclusively as an electoral body, even though this is an element that cannot be forgotten. Indeed, people reflect very little on the fact, too often taken for granted, that parliamentarians, differently from the office-holders of other organs, are appointed by elections. This fact should confer on them a role and an influence that is different from the other organs. This means that just as parliament has been the organ that more than any other has democratised the representation of individuals, its role can also be revitalised by democratising those groups that today perform a function that is increasingly important in political decisions.

In other terms, one is dealing with finding a way for this organism to overcome the very idea, which is also a little obsolete, of 'a minimum democracy in which citizens exercise their sovereignty through an action that lasts a few seconds, repeated some years later'. This means certain really important things: the *first* brings into play the criterion itself of democratic representation which has been the object of suspicion since the outset, but which above all today has become for the most part an expression of 'a democratic aristocracy'. Elections themselves seem to always favour the usual figures, even if they come from other powers whose fame and image, for various reasons, they have been able to exploit. I am thinking here of the very many representatives from the world of the judiciary or from

---

113 P. L. Zampetti, *La democrazia partecipativa e il rinnovamento delle istituzioni*, pp. 16, 34.

that of communications who in exploiting a fame that has already been acquired always begin electoral contexts with an indubitable advantage. It would be appropriate to think of *a period of decantation* in order to annul a facilitation at the outset that makes the struggle an unequal one. The *second* is the personalisation of representation whose risks of sliding into populism are increasingly strong. The *third* relates to the real influence of democratic representation.[114] This is increasingly countered by other powers including ones that stand out less but which are not, because of this, less strong. At least at other moments they have seemed to want to react to an evil other than representation: that of direct democracy in its extreme forms with its risk of creating the so-called tyranny of numbers, against which the American Federalists (amongst others) fought.

It is certainly the case that these risks also derive from a certain involution of parties which have been transformed into 'oligarchies integrated into the state and centres of power', when, instead, they should retrieve their role and avoid a further crumbling of political participation, if not, indeed, disintegration, claiming crucial tasks such as that of a 'democracy of surveillance'.[115] These are tasks that cannot be performed without an ethical vision that was a basis for the birth of certain parties.

Whereas the *legislative* power has to take into account requests relating to a renewed criterion of representation, the *executive* power has to meet a growing need rapidly to provide answers that are able to direct and implement

---

114 Cf. I. Diamanti, 'Prefazione' to B. Manin, *The Principles of Representative Government* (Cambridge University Press, New York, 1997); Italian edition: *Principi del governo rappresentativo*, translated by V. Ottonelli (Il Mulino, Bologna, 2010), pp. VIIff.

115 Cf. on this point P. Rosanvallon, *La contre-démocratie. La politique à l'âge de la défiance*, above all the first part.

decisions. Overall, the executive has to be able to shoulder its responsibilities and respond to the unpostponable request to make the bureaucratic power efficient. This was a power that was born, as Weber pointed out,[116] to rationalise economic life, which today in order to keep pace with frenetic competition has to be able to meet new needs without 'hold-ups' or the loss of time. It is for this reason that an analysis of the executive more than concentrating exclusively on its capacity to be an 'expression of power' should concentrate on what is defined as its 'procedure': 'by this is meant the process involving the implementation of laws, rules and in general all the political decisions of the government'.[117] This means that its assessment must involve above all its efficiency and efficacy. Here it should be assessed not only in relation to the legislative and the judicial powers, as contemporary debates would have us believe, but also with respect to the bureaucracy, which constitutes the other face of the executive. Indeed, 'the relations between the government and the bureaucracy can acquire characteristics that are very different according to the stability-instability, homogeneity-heterogeneity and dynamism-immobility of the governmental system and the forms of recruitment and the level of training and competence of the bureaucracy'.[118] It is specifically on the basis of these principles that the executive can, and must, claim new space in relation to other powers.

The *judicial* power, for its part, arose with a precise intention which by now, at least in theory, is said to have

---

116 On this subject see chap. VIII, 'Bureaucracy: The Pursuit of Efficiency. A Gnoseological problem', in R. Pezzimenti, *Superstructure and Structure. An Essay on the Genesis of Economic Development* (Gracewing, 2015).

117 G. Pasquino, 'Esecutivo', in N. Bobbio, N. Matteucci and G. Pasquino (eds.), *Dizionario di politica*, p. 370.

118 *Ibidem*.

become an inescapable principle of the whole of humanity – to perform in an autonomous way a precise function: the judicial function. This 'essentially involves entrusting the resolution of conflicts between the members of society to impartial third parties who rationally apply general principles that may be written or unwritten'.[119] For this reason, it has to interact with cultures and moralities and therefore with laws that cannot be ignored even if, often, they deserve to be regulated in a suitable way. All discussions about this power, in addition to concentrating on a series of auxiliary measures that are fundamental in applying justice, should concentrate on the need for the impartiality of the holders of this power. Although this is a subject that ends up by having a political value, no less crucial is the question of the time involved in providing justice which can compromise interests of various other kinds. I will now refer briefly to the most relevant: the corporative power of lawyers, which some observers tend to underestimate.

Corporative power[120] is *a power that always* flanked the classic powers and today it flanks the most recent powers as well, even if its presence at some points has been more marked than at others. This is a power that has been overly neglected and often given up as dead only to be always revitalised. Yet it deserves to be remembered, with its new appellation of *'neo-corporative'* as well. Its ganglions are so present in civil society that it determines its decisions and often ends that are not always universally accepted. It is one of the powers that could have been most easily limited but its 'regulation' clashes with a series of consolidated interests and thus ones that are difficult to attack. It is

---

119 A. Marradi, 'Sistema giudiziario', in N. Bobbio, N. Matteucci and G. Pasquino (eds.), *Dizionario di politica*, p. 924.

120 Cf. N. Matteucci, *Lo Stato moderno. Lessico e percorsi* (Il Mulino, Bologna, 1993), chap. VI, pp. 189ff.

curious that everybody sees it as a form of antithesis to so-termed open societies but despite this it is tolerated so as not to go against the consensus of major strata of the population and to avoid their opposition to established power.

2. The fourth power, the fifth power and the two faces of the sixth power

The three classic powers should be flanked by the powers that have gradually become established during modernity so that in addition to the influence that they exercise they have precise rules and roles in order to avoid that they, as well, go beyond their limits and occupy spaces that belong to other powers. I am alluding here to the *fourth and fifth powers*: the press and in general the mass media and means of communication. 'The fifth power, that is to say the TV, is such because in entering every home more than any other power it has an opportunity to shape general feelings and action, direct consumption and behaviour, produce stereotypes or stars, form and educate'.[121] We should remember that the importance of the *fifth power* depends on the fact that today it interprets a *classic* task for political parties – the *capacity to communicate in order to change.* Indeed, it is undoubted that this power '(a) seeks to bring about a change in the other party's position, and (b) does so using propositions that are impersonal or relate to the long-term future'. Whatever the case, this procedure can be defined as 'haggling, in which the participants seek to change each other's positions through rewards or threats'.[122]

---

121 E. Narduzzi, *Sesto potere. Chi governa la società nell'era della tecnologia di massa e dell'innovazione permanente*, p. 7.

122 Cf. B. Manin, *The Principles of Representative Government* (Cambridge University Press, New York, 1997), p. 198.

It is undoubted that all of this requires the criterion of the fullest transparency.

The same criterion of transparency should be applied to the *sixth power* or technological power. Its role has been gradually growing and, from certain points of view, also provoking concern. To say that today there are new forms of power derives from the fact 'that the presence of powers in a society is not static over time'. It is for this reason that there are gradually posed 'new questions and issues relating to their discipline or regulation'. The technological power is today a power that even seems to go beyond that of accompanying 'individuals from the cradle to the grave' because technology seems, paradoxically, to range 'from DNA to beyond the tomb'. Technology is certainly a new phenomenon but also new is the fact that it has in an overbearing way moved out of the sphere of the laboratory where it remained a phenomenon of a few specialists and become a 'mass phenomenon'.[123] There is an increasing wish for technology to become a 'social power'. However, a power becomes 'such only if it is universal in action, democratic in assigning, and specialist in application'. In other terms, technology cannot be viewed as a 'niche phenomenon' because it is directed towards producing novelties and innovations whose utilisation involves everyone. In addition, technology, if we understand things correctly, raises a problem similar to that of the fourth and fifth powers, namely that of 'placing powers of a private matrix at the side of traditional public powers'.[124]

The difficulties encountered in regulating this power, differently from the fourth and fifth powers, lies in the fact that this *sixth* power is by its nature 'global in the sense

---

123 E. Narduzzi, *Sesto potere. Chi governa la società nell'era della tecnologia di massa e dell'innovazione permanente*, pp. 4-5.

124 Cf. *ibid.*, p. 8.

that the results of its activity can contemporaneously be used by more than one society'.[125] This is a power that encounters difficulties in being disciplined because, like financial power, it is transnational in character. It should, however, be observed, as the recent restrictions of the Chinese government have demonstrated, that a strong executive, that is to say one capable of closing the space of the innovations and communications coming from abroad, runs the risk of impeding the use of certain instruments. The same restrictions have occurred from Byelorussia to Thailand, and what has recently taken place in the Maghreb cannot reignite enthusiasm given that the success of some operations is more due to the incapacity of governments to eliminate them than to the capillary activity of those who revolt. These last, in the end – and Libya demonstrates this fact – have placed their hopes more in weapons of allies than in their capacity to communicate and ridicule power. In contrary fashion, the Chinese experience is of the greatest importance because it has finally dampened the enthusiasm of those who dreamed of achieving a new representative democracy.[126] Digital technology not only has not fostered direct democracy – it *has also aggravated new forms of neo-populism* that were already generated and supported by the television.

This does not remove the fact that these technological forms are linked to developments in typical futurology which power, in the broad sense of the term, tends to keep under control. It is certainly no accident that in February 2011 Obama dined with the powerful of the high-tech world on which depends most of the political supremacy of the immediate future.

---

125 *Ibid.*, p. 9.
126 Cf. for the end of this dream: D. Pittèri, *Democrazia elettronica* (Laterza, Rome-Bari, 2002).

The real difficulty, however, appears to be another: this power, which is attractive and meritocratic, is unstable and always 'open to change'. But this is not enough: one is dealing with a power that is able to be rapidly subverted, continuously called to engage in innovation, and closely subject to risk. All of this also depends on the fact that this sixth power 'does not have a precise organisational chart that explains the roles and functions of those who are directly involved'.[127] This brings us back to the ancient problem of controlling – if this is possible – the trend of development, investments and the results of research. Indeed, one cannot ignore how much the so-called *sixth power* is linked to another power – the *commercial power*, which in its turn is connected to the *industrial* and *banking and financial* powers, to which I will refer shortly. In this case, one cannot speak solely of *regulation*: the real question is seeing if such regulation can be *preventive*, as happens with the other powers.

For many, this power, even if it ran the risk of leading to an 'unwanted innovation', could not be regulated along the same lines as the other powers because this would mean inhibiting its possibility of aiming at changing society and its way of life. I will confine myself to saying that this dream, pursued 'by a rather numerous group of scientists',[128] has often generated more problems, often of a dramatic nature, than solutions. For that matter, ever since Comte the constructivist dream has not abandoned us and as today it has become an integral part of our lives it requires that regulation that accompanies every other power.

I would like to be clear upon this point: *regulation is not directed* towards clipping the wings of research. It must, however, be applied to those powers that support it for their

---

127 Cf. E. Narduzzi, *Sesto potere. Chi governa la società nell'era della tecnologia di massa e dell'innovazione permanente*, pp. 11ff.

128 Cf. *Ibid.*, p. 26.

own ends. For that matter, if we think of some of the variants of technological power, such as *cybernetic power*, we have to say that there are authentic world authorities such as Sherry Turkle[129] who evoke the same powers that apply to 'real life'. There is a crucial power that today flanks research – that of lobbies which can be defined as the other face of the *sixth power*. The word 'lobby', with everything that it represents, from interests to pressure groups, despite its history going back about two centuries has always been surrounded (and today more than ever before) by a certain diffidence. Lobbies appeared as an indefinable power, as has been said an *invisible parliament*, a sort of alternative legislative chamber, able to 'decentralise' the democratic system.[130] There can be no doubt that they constitute a power, even though other powers use them, but a power that seems to escape all possible controls, in addition to being a power that is generated with criteria of representation that are not always clear. Reassuring definitions have not helped to overcome the problem. Definitions such as 'lobby'; 'a group expressing an interest or a cause to defend; 'lobbyist' – personnel inside or outside an organisation by which representation is implemented; 'lobbyism' – the set of techniques and activities that allows the political representation of interests'.[131] This means that there is no

---

129 Of the numerous texts by Sherry Turale, I here refer the reader to some of the most recent: *Alone Together: Why We Expect More from Technology and Less from Each Other* (Basic Books, New York, January 2011); *Simulation and Its Discontents* (MIT Press, Cambridge, MA, 2009); *The Second Self: Computers and the Human Spirit*, Twentieth Anniversary edition, including new introduction, epilogue, and notes (MIT Press, Cambridge, MA, 2005).

130 Cf. M. Franco, *Lobby: il Parlamento invisibile. Candidati, gruppi di pressione e finanziamenti elettorali nell'America degli anni '80* (Il Sole 24 Ore, Milan, 1988).

131 G. Graziano, *Le lobbies* (Laterza, Rome-Bari, 2002), p. 22.

definition that can avoid certain basic fears, above all if one takes into account that by 'lobbying' is meant the possibility of transmitting 'messages from a pressure group to decision-makers through specialised representatives'.[132] It is certainly the case that here as well the word 'representatives' seems to move out of the classic canons with which it has been considered, not least because, when speaking about representatives, it is always borne in mind that they have to be accountable, at the least to the represented.

To these perplexities can be added others that are no less disquieting. The fact is that professional prestige does not always manage to transform the *reputations of people*. Indeed, one cannot forget that in the eyes of public opinion lobbyists engage in activity that is not always clear and definable. This not only points to the close connection that exists between this phenomenon and public opinion. It also emphasises the dangers that in the view of the latter this phenomenon represents for democracy.[133] The belief (advanced by Mazzei) that lobbies support civil society against the excessive power of the state, and thus find fertile terrain where political systems are strong, is not enough to reassure the fearful. They are thus a physiological moment of a political system, even if they end up by becoming pathological 'when they are not placed in a condition to operate correctly and with transparency'.[134] To say that lobbyists have to have particular requirements to operate

---

132 Cf. G. Pasquino, 'Gruppi di pressione', in N. Bobbio, N. Matteucci ad G. Pasquino (eds.), *Dizionario di politica*.

133 Cf. M. Spalletta, *Comunicare responsabilmente. Etica e deontologie dell'informazione e della comunicazione* (Rubbettino Editore, Soveria Mannelli, 2010), pp. 169-170.

134 Cf. G. Mazzei, *Lobby della trasparenza. Manuale di relazioni istituzionali* (Centro di documentazione giornalistica, Rome, 2006), pp. 28, 32; quoted from the text of M. Spalletta cited in footnote 133.

well does not remove the fact that this 'fertile terrain' in which they are called to operate seems to be a terrain with boundaries that are not always well defined, where, that is, they are not obscure.

It should certainly also be said that some fears at times are not only unfounded but also harbour a vision of politics that is probably more dangerous and typical of those (still imbued with certain ideologies) who presume or dream of a 'neutrality' in political decisions, if not indeed an 'infallibility' of institutions. They regard lobbies as useless because they believe that politics can, and knows how to, do everything on its own. Hence it is right to seek from lobbyists *professionalism*, *transparency* and *honesty*.[135] Given, however, that the future of individual lobbyists depends on their professionalism, there remains, if anything, the question of controlling aspects such as transparency. Indeed, it is the case that although a constant updating is fundamental in defeating superficiality, opportunism and demagoguery, on the basis of which it would be impossible to direct effective initiatives, the fact remains that lobbies embody a 'democracy of interests'[136] which in themselves do not constitute an evil but anyway require limits and controls. The problem becomes crucial when lobbies seek special answers to problems that themselves are not special, when, that is to say, they should seek to express shared answers to problems that affect everyone – answers that could instead damage those groups that pay lobbies to obtain particular results.

Thus it is that in addition to the so-termed deontological approach, to which reference has just been made, based

---

135 Cf. M. Spalletta, *Comunicare responsabilmente. Etica e deontologie dell'informazione e della comunicazione*, pp. 171ff.

136 Cf. P. Trupia, *La democrazia degli interessi: lobby e decisione collettiva* (Il Sole 24 Ore, Milan, 1989), quoted in the text of M. Spalletta.

upon *professionalism*, *transparency* and *honesty*, lobbyists should also be required to have *impartiality*. This is easier to achieve in those lobbyists who when they communicate their name always add the organisation for which they work.[137] However, the incontestable fact remains that the organisation for which they work, because it pays, expects certain results that could at the least undermine their impartiality.

Certain difficulties have been well understood by the European Union which when referring to *honesty* established that a lobbyist must avoid inducing third parties or personnel of the EU into error. When emphasising *integrity* it observed that a lobbyist cannot induce the functionaries of the EU to contravene measures and rules relating to conduct. However, the problem remains that where this is not done the set of sanctions is clouded, not to say a matter of wishful thinking.[138] This confirms the need to achieve a more serious definition of a power that has become notably relevant today.

3. The transformation and the growing role of other powers

In addition to the powers that have already been examined there exist other powers that from certain points of view are more traditional but which hitherto have been held at times to be immune to controls. I am thinking of *commercial* power. Who can deny that a national union of industrialists has an enormous influence in the political affairs of a modern State? Very precise limits apply to this power as well – limits *obviously* of a juridical nature – in order to avoid the always recurring risk of experiencing a new and

---

137 Cf. M. Spalletta, *Comunicare responsabilmente. Etica e deontologie dell'informazione e della comunicazione*, p. 191.

138 Cf. *Ibid.*, p. 192.

dangerous statism. And this for the further reason that never as much as before do 'the protection of the interests of one's own *category* take place in the domain of a more general interest'. Businessmen, therefore, 'also perceive [or should perceive] the responsibility of collective interests and not only those of their own company and their own category'.[139] All of this must be connected to the great lesson of Tocqueville who argued that various groups or associations should have the opportunity to be represented so as to pursue their own interests in clear, legal and universally recognised ways. For this reason, businessmen must have their own organs of representation that are autonomous and based upon the consensus of their grassroots, creating those intermediate bodies which are so useful for the growth of a society that is authentically democratic.[140] To do this they have to avoid the risk – which is typical of other forces such as trade unions – of being litigious and of a fragmentation that can frustrate proposals and demands addressed to other powers.[141] They must also avoid dangerous intrusions into their field of action which can mean the loss of their sense of limits. A president of a national union of industrialists has a role and social and economic influence that is evident to us all and can certainly not accept that he should be offered, specifically while he has that role, the acceptance of posts typical of the executive, as we have recently witnessed in Italy. No authentically balanced and 'limited' system can

---

139 L. Abete, 'Prefazione' to P. Nicoletti, *I sistemi di rappresentanza degli interessi economici in Italia* (Luiss University Press, Rome, 2001), p. 9. The text in squared brackets is mine.

140 Cf. G. De Rita, 'Prefazione', to R. Melchionna, *Il retrobottega del sistema rappresentativo italiano (1958-1987)* (Rubbettino Editore, Soveria Mannelli, 2007).

141 Cf. P. Nicoletti, *I sistemi di rappresentanza degli interessi economici in Italia*, p. 32.

accept these kinds of solutions. Here, as well, one should think of a *period of decantation*, as I have already suggested in the case of some media figures.

It is right to remember that in order to avoid such contradictions one should 'foster the development of the culture of responsibility within the system of representation', without failing to mention that this culture, in addition to the vertical model which has always been implemented, should also aim at 'a model of territorial coalition, that is to say *horizontal* representation in the local area'.[142] However, this applies to every power that is at work in the domain of civil society and, anyway, does not free us from the need to be vigilant.

All of this becomes extremely necessary at a time when many governments are engaged in a process of privatisation that is also strongly changing the role of decision-making. This is a development where 'institutional relationships, in relation to which European and regional/local levels have adopted a key role at the side of the role of the State'[143] would facilitate a new advance towards the democracy of intermediate bodies and authentic representation. A more streamlined and effective business system is required in the face of a growing simplification of the political framework. Treu has rightly observed[144] that the strengthening of bipolarity imposes new imperatives on the world of business 'with more selective functions and with a greater taking on of responsibility towards the political framework'.

It is clear that connected to the commercial power there is also the *banking* power and this is closely intertwined with the *financial* power whose meanders are often very obscure

---

142 Ibid., pp. 35, 39.

143 *Ibid.*, p. 43.

144 Cf. T. Treu, 'Un nuovo associazionismo imprenditoriale?', in *Diritto delle Relazioni Industriali*, n. 1, 2006.

but whose importance cannot be doubted by anybody. The conflicts of interest that are present in this power go beyond national interests and often escape rules and controls. From this comes the need – to be looked for above all in supra-national domains – to discipline some subjects of a relevance that is not only economic in character.

The power of *trade unions*, whose historical role, like its slow crumbling due to an increasingly precarious unity, is undoubted, is opposed to the power of business. For a long period the role of trade unions was crucial but not completely autonomous because it was performed in obedience to party institutions. Indeed, there was a period, like that of the post-war years, and in certain countries as long as there was a strongly ideological vision, when 'the primacy of the action of parties in relation to social dynamics' was witnessed. This was a period when one could even talk about a 'state of parties'.[145] Only with the years that preceded the crisis of the Soviet bloc did the situation emerge of 'seeing trade unions as a social subject which through the enlargement of its contractual and negotiating action relating to the modification of economic realities... [could be] involved in the general political process of democratisation',[146] thereby coming to address questions

---

145 A. Ciampani, 'Movimento sindacale e partiti politici nel sistema democratico dell'Italia repubblicana', in *Annali 2005-2006*, edited by G. Ignesti (Giappichelli Editore, Turin, 2007), p. 14. On this subject see also P. Scoppola, *La Repubblica dei partiti. Profilo storico della democrazia in Italia 1945-199* (Il Mulino, Bologna, 1991).

146 A. Ciampani, 'Movimento sindacale e partiti politici nel sistema democratico dell'Italia repubblicana', p. 16. The text in squared brackets is mine. The author here refers to V. Saba, *Sindacalismo*, in *Dizionario delle idee politiche*, edited by E. Berti and G. Campanili (AVE, Rome, 1994), pp. 771-784; G. Marongiu, *La democrazia come problema. I.2 Diritto, amministrazione ed economia* (Il Mulino, Bologna, 1994).

which also touched upon the democratic principles of the economy itself.

This was a new kind of trade unionism, therefore, created, as well, by the irreversible crisis of a Left based upon the Soviet Union and the control that this wielded over workers' movements, as has been rather well demonstrated by a significant number of sociological analyses.[147] This was a question that affected above all those countries such as Italy, France and Spain where Communist Parties were rather strong. One could therefore say that the trade union movement has undergone an authentic journey of emancipation, placing itself as an autonomous subject in a pluralistic system of political and economic relationships in an increasingly complex reality, such as we have today, wanting, however, to make a contribution 'to the increasingly involved process of the governance of society'.[148] For this reason, trade unions have acquired a new role and thus a new power which, although experiencing today a certain waning, deserves to be regulated like other powers.

From what has been said, one can understand that it is no longer sufficient to address in classic terms the whole question of the limitation of powers. We are dealing with a problem that is posing new challenges for political theory and political practices. It is advisable not to fall into the error of underestimating or postponing such problems, occupied as we are, unfortunately, with a contingent dimension that, above all in politics, does to seem to leave room for farsighted projects. The risk of this is that we will no longer being able to understand crucial aspects of the historical-social future.

---

147 Cf., for example, A. Touraine, *Critique de la modernité* (Librairie Arthème Fayard, Paris, 1992); Italian edition: *Critica della Modernità*, translated by F. Siriana, (Il Saggiatore, Milan, 1997), pp. 280 ff.

148 Cf. A. Ciampani, *Movimento sindacale e partiti politici nel sistema democratico dell'Italia repubblicana*, pp. 23ff and p. 43.

VIII. MORE ON THE DIVISION OF POWERS

After what was said in the previous chapter, it is now appropriate to return to the already cited study of Ackerman. When speaking about the division of powers, this American scholar seeks to restore a leading role to the people by limiting the power of those who represent them, namely parliament, as well. The aim is 'the protection and enhancement of fundamental rights. Without these, democratic rule and professional administration can readily become engines of tyranny'. One is dealing, therefore, with placing limits on classic parliamentarianism. What is needed, therefore, is to find new ways by which 'the lawmaking powers of parliament may be constrained by other institutions of democratic self-government, including popular referenda on the national level and the representation of provincial governments in federal systems.[149] This second system is defined by the author as a 'one-and-a-half house'.

As far as I am concerned, I believe that it is appropriate to emphasise that even referendums, and not only referendums, must have limits. Ackerman seems to admit this when he observes that Germany itself, probably because of the 'Nazi disaster', has avoided the institution of the referendum 'like the plague'. He then adds that constitutional structures of a federal kind in some countries 'were not generated *from below* by preexisting states moving in the direction of federal union'. They evolved out of structures 'imposed *from above* by constitutional designers convinced of the

---

[149] B. Ackerman, 'The New Separation of Power', p. 640.

rational superiority of the Westminster model'.[150] Here, as well, I feel that I should add that not everything that arises from the grassroots necessarily respects fundamental rights. From the *grassroots*, as in the French Revolution, was generated that dangerous reality of self-appointed assemblies that silenced a significant number of critical voices.

This is a problem of enormous importance that has led some (for example Hoppe)[151] to speak about the failure of democracy. This pessimistic position does not derive only from some unfortunate results: it also arises from evidently insufficient theoretical premises. 'Hence his insistence on the need for a *theory a priori*, that is to say propositions that assert something that is valid about reality'.[152] One is dealing not only, as is evident, with an anti-utilitarian position but also with a conviction directed towards establishing principles that are not easy to remove – in my point of view rights that are not negotiable – on which to found democratic bases capable of resisting whims or fashions. This was also the conviction of Burke, to which I will return shortly.

The dangers that derive from knowing how to oppose whims and fashions seems to me, however, perceived by Ackerman when he argues that democratic legitimacy must be limited 'by the previous decisions of the people rendered through serial referenda and enforced by a constitutional court'. In addition, this popular power 'may also be checked by a subordinate federal senate or a more powerful second

---

150 *Ibid.*, p. 670

151 Cf. H.H. Hoppe, *Democracy: The God That Failed* (Transaction Publishers through Nabu International Literary Agency, 2001).

152 R. Cubeddu, 'Prefazione' to the Italian edition of H. H. HOPPE, *Democracy: The God That Failed*, translated by A. Mingardi (Liberilibri, Macerata, 2005), p. XIX.

chamber organized on national lines'. All of this is said, obviously, without forgetting that when one speaks about fundamental rights the whole of the discussion 'depends on how one defines the fundamental'.[153] To sum up, the danger that any power can degenerate exists: this cannot in any way be ignored or underestimated.

Similarly, limits that according to some are other limits, which if we have to call them such I would prefer to define as *removable limits*, cannot be ignored. These are the limits of poverty, of ignorance and of prejudice. Indeed, these often compromise other fundamental limits. Without mentioning that often these are *limits* that classes, States and other forms of interested powers do everything not to remove.

But let us remain with the popular will which can take exaggerated forms. Compagna, citing Talmon, reminds us of a classic Jacobin approach: 'The more the forms of popular sovereignty are extreme, the more procedure is democratic, the more one can be certain of unanimity'.[154] This, which is certainly an insinuation against Rousseau, tends to highlight how popular sovereignty, as well, must be subject to limits.

Usually, in many cases, the first victim of these extremes is specifically that liberalism in the name of which people speak and which, perhaps in good faith, people try to defend. The so-termed liberalism of Sieyès should have taught us something here. 'His was a monolithic liberalism, hostile (it does not matter with which and how many good reasons) to pluralism. It is no accident that he came to argue that *l'intérêt personnel n'est point à craindre*. This was a personal interest that should have been pursued in private, *il est isolé chacun*

---

153 B. Ackerman, 'The New Separation of Power', pp. 723, 718.

154 L. Compagna, *L'idea dei partiti da Hobbes a Burke* (Città Nuova Editrice, Rome, 2008), p. 166.

a le sien. In his view it was a gross error to have it prevail at a public level: there it was not even possible to present it and support it. 'Hence the implacable rejection' of the very idea of a party'.[155] Although paradoxical, this position of revolutionary France was one that was rather similar to that of contemporary China. Liberalism in the economic-social context; statism in the political-institutional context.

This idea of Rousseau, from an anthropological point of view, appears to have been totally upturned by Burke for whom 'artificial society arises, in the ultimate analysis, from man's radical incapacity to know how to identify his limit'.[156] There is no turning of natural society into myth through an exaltation of the idea of the *noble savage*. On the contrary, when artificial society, or to put it better political society, breaks the founding limits that characterise it, one returns, not always being aware of this, to natural society.

Indeed, one returns to a form of government that Burke characterises with a happy phrase. He argues that politics and its form of government becomes 'occasional', uncertain from every point of view.[157] An 'essentially *capricious* will' is expressed again, the will that characterises despotism. It could not be otherwise given that the individual goes back to finding himself 'alone, without the possibility of help, in the face of the absoluteness of political power'. Hence the instability and the constant changeability of the ends

---

155 *Ibid.*, p. 172. The quotations in French are from Sieyès E.-J., *Qu'est-ce que le tiers* état? (*Essai sur les privilèges*, au Siège de la Société, Paris, 1888).

156 M. D'Addio, *Natura e società nel pensiero di Edmund Burke* (Giuffrè Editore, Milan, 2008), p. 41. For the statements of Burke see E. Burke, *A Vindication of Natural Society, The Writings and Speeches of Edmund Burke*, general editor Paul Langford, vol. I, *The Early Writings*, edited by T. O. McLoughin and James T. Boulton (Clarendon Press, Oxford, 1997), pp. 138-139.

157 Cf. E. Burke, *A Vindication of Natural Society*, p. 155.

towards which political action should tend.¹⁵⁸ This last also becomes in this way 'occasional'. With the founding limits of a political society no longer there, all the other limits also fall, beginning with the ethical limits and ending with the rational limits, given that *each power expresses its rationality which dissolves with the disappearance of a sense of limits*.

Let us return at this point to the solution posed by Ackerman when he speaks about a 'one-and-half house', that is to say a federal senate subordinated to a national chamber of deputies. A senate understood in this way does not seem to me an institution that one could improvise in any country. 'Federal' senators have a sense when they express a direct relationship with the land and the population that they represent. For this reason, it seems to me that it does not have much sense to reduce the senate to a 'Chamber of Ambassadors' in the sense of positing that a 'Constitution may authorise state governments to appoint their representatives directly to seats in one or another federal institution' as takes place with 'the Council of the European Union'.¹⁵⁹ I believe that such a formula is a poor qualification for a power and affects in a serious way its effective capacity to be representative.

An infinity of legal, political and other observations have been made about representation. Perhaps it is appropriate to start with a simple etymological meaning of the Latin verb '*repraesentare*'. One is dealing here with 'making present again'; this is its 'political use in the sense of acting as subject authorised or deputed by someone'. Oliver Cromwell referred to this when he said in a speech to members of parliament that he had looked to their safety and the safety of those that they represented. Leoni himself

---

158 Cf. M. D'Addio, *Natura e società nel pensiero di Edmund Burke*, p. 46.
159 B. Ackerman, 'The New Separation of Power', pp. 678-679.

reminds us of the antiquity of this concept but also, we may say, of its function. The Roman jurist Pomponius, in a fragment of the *Digest*, observed: 'The Senate was led to take on responsibility for legislation because of the difficulty of bringing together the plebs and because of the greater difficulty of holding an assembly of the vast multitude of the entire electorate'. The discourse became different when the need was affirmed not only to have representatives of the people but also of various minorities. This need became established in the Middle Ages when, as Gierke observes, in the Church as well canonists believed 'that minorities had certain undeniable rights and that questions of faith could not be decided by simple majorities'.[160] We here encounter one of those non-negotiable rights that no power can ever call into question.

When it comes to a senate or upper chamber, we should remember, with Montesquieu, that they represent a history, a tradition, a culture and a spirit. It is precisely this last that has been badly interpreted, otherwise we should ask ourselves why the liberal system developed only in some States and not in others,[161] and as a consequence, with it, the separation of powers. One ought to say the same about the federal system which to survive must make *union* and *autonomy* co-exist. Both these characteristics are the outcome of culture but it should be emphasised that although the *second* (autonomy) allows a federal system to be such, it is the *first* (union) that enables it to survive and not to disintegrate.

---

160 Cf. B. Leoni, *Freedom and the Law* (Liberty Press, Indianapolis, 1991); Italian edition: M. C. Pievatolo, *La libertà e la legge* (Liberilibri, Macerata, 2000), pp. 131ff. The work of the German scholar referred to is the English edition O. Gierke, *Political Theories of the Middle Age*, translation by Maitland (Cambridge University Press, Cambridge, 1922).

161 Cf. the first chapter of this study.

If one approaches politics from a cultural perspective, it should be said that it is absolutely not enough to pass good laws for these to be applied well when there is no tradition able to implement them or, even worse, when the ability to implement them has ended. In this, I can agree with Ackerman when he observes: 'The result is a burst of legislation that seeks to express long-suppressed ideas and beliefs'. This means that legislative activity, as well, displays intrinsic limits. Indeed, it absolutely must display them if a democracy does not want to experience one of its most dangerous defects – legislative demagoguery. This occurs, for example, when, near to elections 'the government will favour lawmaking initiatives strong in symbolic statement'[162] and one must absolutely not fall back on arguing, as is the case with some pessimists, that this is the price that a democracy has to pay.

More than paying the price of democracy, it seems that parliamentary systems have to pay the price of governability 'by awarding plenary lawmaking authority to the victors regardless of the quality of their electoral majority'. It is for this reason that the most developed democracies seek to change the rules of the democratic game with a qualified majority, specifically to avoid each winner rewriting the rules according to their own needs and perspectives. If this is not done, a problem presents itself that goes beyond the political dimension alone. To ensure the actuation and the working of the system, certain politicians could act by 'creating their own hyperpoliticised mini-bureaucracies'. The decisions of such bureaucracies would tend to exclude the experience of very many capable functionaries and would be taken 'by callow flunkies eager to curry favor with their bosses and the special interests that support

---

162 B. Ackerman, 'The New Separation of Power', p. 651.

them'.¹⁶³ It is probably from here that we have to start in order to examine what people are beginning to define as the 'mediocrity of democracies'. Perhaps we need to go back to thinking about the reflections of Weber¹⁶⁴ on bureaucracy and then go beyond them because today they are no longer sufficient.

The problem of bureaucracy is a crucial problem of contemporary democracies and it is one that is not envisaged by various Constitutions. These have always placed it within the executive power and do not envisage collusions or risks in relation to it – first of all that of inefficiency. Nobody can deny that when other powers, including the legislature not to speak of the executive, have wanted to take specific decisions excluding the experience of experts in the field, they have often taken ineffective decisions.

In addition, the real problem is that bureaucracy itself, as the totalitarian systems demonstrated, in identifying itself with the executive has ended up by prevailing over individual liberties. This has meant the diminution of the protection of the needs of individuals and an inability to solve their disputes, as well as an increase in expenditure on the judicial system and a decrease in its quality.¹⁶⁵ This phenomenon can also be encountered in those democratic States where bureaucracy is not very efficient.

From what has been observed here, a further problem emerges which, however, deserves separate treatment¹⁶⁶

---

163 *Ibid.*, pp. 664, 687.

164 I have already addressed thus question: cf. R. Pezzimenti, *Politics and Economics. An Essay on the Genesis of Economic Development* (Gracewing Fowler Wright Books, Leominster, 2004), chap. VIII.

165 Cf. H.H. Hoppe, *Democracy: The God that Failed*, 13.III.

166 I referred to this question in my *Politics and Economics. An Essay on the Genesis of Economic Development*. I am preparing a new expanded edition of this work in order to give this subject the space it deserves.

and should be highlighted. Hayek[167] rightly observed that Schumpeter[168] had the impression – I would say the certainty – that a system based upon the freedom of the market was doomed. He thought that although it could be seen as the best for the majority of people, it would be superseded by a socialist view of the economy which, although unable to keep promises and meet the expectations of people, was destined to succeed because it would provide greater security.

It is certainly the case that the observations of Hayek and Schumpeter deserve attention, not least in relation to the management and the division of power. The democratic management of a socio-political entity immediately leads us to ask who are regarded as 'the members' of such organizations for whom a share in their direction is claimed. Can we consider 'members of a hospital, or an hotel, or a club, a teaching institution or a department store' only those who work in such institutions or also those who use them or those who provide what is needed to produce services? This question requires a clarification of the very concept of democracy.[169] How should decisions in such institutions be taken?

In the case of some decisions, for example medical treatment, a decision certainly cannot be taken by majority vote. The case cited above is not exceptional because in bureaucracies it occurs more than can be imagined. Perhaps the ancient Greeks sensed this problem and to the point

---

167 Cf. F.A. Von Hayek, *Law, Legislation and Liberty*, volume 3, *The Political Order of a Free People* (The University of Chicago, Chicago, Phoenix edition, 1981), p. 2.

168 Cf. on this subject above all but not only J.A. Schumpeter, *Capitalism, Socialism and Democracy*, first edtion of 1942, third edition of 1950.

169 Cf. F.A. Von Hayek, *Law, Legislation and Liberty*, volume 3, *The Political Order of a Free People*, pp. 38-39.

that democracy did not always for them have a positive meaning. What matters for us is that the rules relating to access to management in the sphere of bureaucracy should be really democratic, for example the possible removal of the incompetent and the dishonest. It is above all this last aspect that does not appear to be clear, but it is here that one measures the real democratic character of a system and the transparency of powers. Not least because it is specifically from competence and honesty that a *correct management* of the *common good* comes.

IX. THE COMMON GOOD AND ITS VALUES

Populism is a serious phenomenon that should be understood at the level of its causes for it to be addressed and contained. Yascha Mounk in her *The People vs. Democracy*, in the dense 'Introduction' where she speaks about what she defines as lost illusions,[170] reminds us that a first element that should be borne in mind is the goal of a growing economy. As long as the economic system was in expansion there were those, like Francis Fukuyama,[171] who argued that democracy would triumph easily. This observation may be in part true but I believe that it is not completely exhaustive.

1. Towards a real retrieval of the common good

It should also be borne in mind that the tyranny of the majority, which if understood correctly is transformed into tyranny *tout court*, is always just behind the corner of any democracy that does not adhere fully to its premises. For example, as Mounk argues, democracies of a liberal kind cannot ignore those mechanisms that impede the various parties from accumulating too much – not to say all – power. This is the way to proceed towards that democracy without

---

170 Cf. Y. Mounk, *The People vs. Democracy*; Italian edition: *Popolo vs Democrazia. Dalla cittadinanza alla dittatura elettorale* (Feltrinelli Editore, Milan, 2018).

171 Cf. F. Fukayama, *The End of History and the Last Man* (A Division of Macmillan Inc., New York, 1992).

rights that should belong to everyone but which, instead, are solely in the hands of the holders of power. This is *paradoxical* but behind populism there is the erroneous idea that the people are the custodians of all powers, whereas, in opposite fashion, it is precisely the people that increasingly have less say in deciding matters.

When we speak about liberalism, the liberalism that generated the so-termed liberal democracies, we should bear in mind that we have here a term that is to say the least 'encyclopaedic' and the outcome of a long gestation.[172] It is clear, therefore, as I observed in the previous chapter, that one of the problems to be addressed is that of the powers, some of which today are out of control because they have not been adequately delineated. In addition, one of the cardinal points of the democratic system is that it is made up of parties[173] and these need to be revitalised and never put to one side.

Mounk also reminds us of the need for an 'inclusive patriotism'. One is dealing here with a decisive factor based, however, on concrete facts that are really inclusive and not based on rhetorical questions and issues such as, for example, fake tolerance, but on a renewed civic sense accompanied by serious *civic education, housing policy* and a real *common good*. These are subjects that ward off what Michael Billig[174] defined as 'banal nationalism'.

---

172 For the difficult pathway of liberalism see R. Pezzimenti, *The Open Society along the Arduous Path of Modernity, with Letters from Isaiah Berlin and Hilary Putnam*, and *The Open Society and its Friends, with Letters from Isaiah Berlin and Karl R. Popper*, an expanded version of the previous edition in English published with the same publisher in 1997. On the same subject see the first chapter of my *The Political Thought of Lord Acton* (Gracewing, Leominster, 2001 and the first chapter of my *Storia e politica nella riflessione di Jaime Balmes* (Aracne, Rome, 1999.

173 Cf. L. Compagna, *L'idea dei partiti da Hobbes a Burke*.

174 Cf. M. Billig, *Banal Nationalism* (Sage Publications, London, 1995).

As regards *civic education*, I would like to recall the amazement of Polybius, who came from a world of disintegrating institutions, when during the greatest splendour of the Republic he saw that children in all the federal cities passed their first year of school not in learning to read and write but in learning by heart the *Twelve Tables* (the foundation of the institutions of the Republic).[175] No less important is the question of *housing*. Above all in Europe, and I would say in Italy, the prices of homes in central areas have become prohibitive for many young people. Our cities are losing their souls and forcing local inhabitants to live far away and to live lives that are certainly not easy. Areas such as Trastevere in Rome or Porta Romana in Milan have steadily witnessed the disappearance of their traditional inhabitants who, uprooted from their customs, habits and language, in significant numbers survive with nostalgia and often anger. The *common good* requires a separate analysis.

2. *Values and the common good*[176]

It may appear a contradiction to speak today about 'values and the common good' in a context, such as the European context, which is increasingly linked to the idea of the liquid society. Values, in fact, provide an idea of stability, of strong ties, whereas in this 'in many ways novel, phase in the history of modernity' everything that is fluid, liquid and transitory seems to prevail. Everything changes rapidly to the point that at the end of the last century Ulrich Beck argued that today one should speak about 'zombie

---

175 Cf. R. Pezzimenti, *The Open Society and its Friends, with Letters from Isaiah Berlin and Karl R. Popper*, pp. 35-39.

176 Cf. R. Pezzimenti, *Ethics: the Challenges of Modernity* (Gracewing, Fowler Wright Books, Leominster, 2013), especially the second part, where I address this subject in greater depth.

categories' and 'zombie institutions' which 'are dead and still alive'. The same power, understood in the traditional sense, seems today to be related to the ancient model of 'absent landlords'.[177] One of the reasons why modern institutions, including ones that are representative, are in a state of crisis lies in the fact that citizens choose people as their representatives who are increasingly unimportant.

This could appear a contradiction but if we understand the question aright such is not the case. Indeed, it is specifically those who speak about a liquid society who invoke the need for the values of the common good. Some people, to describe this situation, have spoken about a momentary eclipse of values and employed the image of 'sailors bewitched by the witch Circe and changed into pigs'. Ulysses tried to turn these pigs back into men but it was difficult to overcome their resistance. When his friend Elpenor emerged from one of the animals he did nothing else but insult Ulysses. A scoundrel – why had he done that? Ulysses could not even imagine "I was so happy, I could wallow in the mud and bask in the sunshine. I could gobble and guzzle, grunt and squeak, and be free from meditations and doubts... Why did you come?"[178] It appears that there is a well-defined wish to go back to being pigs: the wish to think exclusively of one's own individual interests. This is the end of man as a social and relational being, who, indeed, returns in a selfish way to thinking of himself.

These attempts at ambivalence, at the what is contingent, at recalcitrance (and one should add at constructivism, to which a certain kind of capitalism has not been extraneous), which are so frequent in post-modern culture, certainly find their justification in the pan-rationalist attempts that underpinned the totalitarian regimes of the twentieth

---

177 Cf. Z. Bauman, *Liquid Modernity*, pp. 2, 6.

178 *Ibid.*, p. 18.

century and generated an individualism closed up in itself and of a strongly selfish character. But when we speak about *values* and the *common good* it should be said – at the right moment everybody should recognise this – that they are founded on something that is very different: above all else on another rationality that is well aware of its limitations and for this reason, in essential terms, accepted by everyone. Paradoxically, Bauman himself arrived at this conclusion and could not fail to argue: 'Today there is a crisis of values, without which it is impossible to have cohesion with peace. Without these values it is inconceivable to have a life worthy of being lived'.[179] Georg Simmel argues that values are valuable when they are acquired,[180] it would be fitting to say lived and borne witness to, otherwise they become light, insignificant, like being itself. It would be easy at this point to paraphrase Milan Kundera with his *unbearable lightness of being*.

The desperation – not to say tragedy – of those who experienced totalitarianism sprang from the fact (in itself self-evident) that in those systems one of the cardinal aspects of the European tradition had been eliminated, we could say one of its fundamental values: the fact that power must be the expression of the community that it represents and thus never higher than that community, its needs and its will. This is what forms of authoritarianism and totalitarianism tried to make people forget. But is this not a primary value which even those who exalt contemporary liquid societies certainly do not want to forget?

---

179 Z. Bauman, *Lo spirito e il clic. La società contemporanea fra frenesia e bisogno di speranza*, 'Introduzione' by Riccardo Mazzeo (Edizioni San Paolo, Cinisello Balsamo, 2013), p. 23. This was a paper given by Bauman at the seventh Bibical Festival of Vicenza of which there is no translation in English authorized by San Paolo.

180 Cf. above all else, but not only, G. Simmel, *Das problem der historischen Zeit* (Reuther und Reichard, Berlin, 1916).

All of this is certainly not sufficient when the common good is spoken about. Indeed, one cannot ignore that as early as the Middle Ages Aquinas himself pointed to living well, that is to say living in accord with the virtues, as the purpose of the common good. These are virtues that cannot and must not, in this case, be understood as the only virtues that can be identified. To live well together we also need the virtues that are socially shared, accepted and lived out. It could not be otherwise if one thinks that the *resources* that are available to achieve the common good are always *limited*. Those who do not have this view not only deceive themselves when they imagine an impossible earthly paradise – they also further impoverish the community by not living with parsimony, trying to avoid waste, an element that we are in particular not careful about, thereby highlighting on a number of occasions a particular selfishness that even runs the risk of obtuseness.

This is why the common good must overcome the individualistic approach; it must respect the person who because of a precise cultural approach is a different reality to the individual and not only from an etymological point of view. The *individual*, indeed, is always seen as replaceable when it comes to the function that he performs. The *person*, instead, is a *unicum*, an *irreplaceable* reality because an irreplaceable entity. The individual and the person are not separate things – they are distinct things. A human being is a whole; the ontological unity of a human being cannot be divided in two. This means that society is also a unity of persons and not only of individuals. For that matter, this conclusion, which was already perceived by the Roman world when it argued that the definition of 'political animal' went straight to the citizen who had to be understood – specifically because of the multiplicity and the riches of their actions – as a 'social animal'.

From this point of view, it appears clear that the idea of the common good invokes a social criterion. People are called to solve their most urgent problems together, with each person making their own irremovable contribution. This is because 'the problems to which we are exposed are socially produced problems, and these problems, precisely because of the fact that they are socially produced, can be solved only in society',[181] that is to say in common.

The social common good, therefore, is broader than the political common good and even more exhaustive. Indeed, the social common good is extremely variegated and aggregates various common goods that individual societies – with their rules – seek to attain. The social common good constitutes the end of different societies, the purpose for which they give themselves rules. These rules, although they can change over time, constitute the limit of, and the guarantee for, their functioning. The world of sport can offer us numerous examples here. Those who want to play basketball join a club with its own rules and goals. A basketball player cannot seek to play according to the rules of rugby. If that is what he wants, he has to go to a club that has different goals and rules.

Only in this way can one achieve the integration of the individual and the group. Integration has a strong social value. But a person, to achieve this goal, needs an enhancement based on a very special cultural dimension: a unique atmosphere able to highlight how the good of the community can in certain circumstances, and given certain requirements, be understood as being higher than the good of the individual. This, however, is not enough. Any discourse relating to the common good must avoid disappointments and conflicts that impede its attainment. For this reason,

---

181 Z. Bauman, *Lo spirito e il clic. La società contemporanea fra frenesia e bisogno di speranza*, p. 26.

the common good, whether social or political, must be *appetising* for a plurality of people and above all *attainable* through social organisation. We can say therefore that one must tend towards an *optimal* and *possible* common good. This means that the common good is always capable of being enhanced and can never be seen as perfect, in the way, for example, that totalitarian systems did.

This fact of social organisation is of the greatest importance if we want to avoid sliding into that totalitarian vision in which the state is everything and individuals – in this case not persons – are only fulfilled within it. In this case, the political common good becomes broader and includes the social common good, whereas, instead, the opposite should be the case. We should also consider the fact that there are goods that cannot be attained in the political dimension. This is an aspect that highlights once again how the person is a unique and not repeatable entity.

Starting from these premises, we can return to the analysis of the values of the common good. 'Values' could be seen as an out-of date term, above all in a society that is liquid, but if we see things aright it is not values that are subject to crisis but rather a set of pseudo-values to which individuals – forgetting the common good – have selfishly tied themselves. An incontestable value has already been identified – the fact that a power must be the expression of the community that it represents and therefore never superior to it, its needs and its will. This is what forms of authoritarianism and totalitarianism tried to make people forget. In addition to this, we can identify values that are instrumental, functional and specific when it comes to the common good.[182] Choices relating to the order of importance of such values can vary from culture to culture, from age

---

182 Cf. A. M. Quintas, *Analisi del bene comune*, second edition (Bulzoni Editore, Rome, 1979).

to age, but the essential character of their relevance is not called into question by anybody.

Amongst the *instrumental values*, the economic values that arise from one's own labour stand out. It is incontestable that *work* is a characterising element of participation in the common good. Those who do not work are forced not only to live by expedients but also not to plan their future lives. For this reason, democratic governments pay especial attention to the question of employment, as the Italian Constitution emphasises at its beginning.

The gamut of *functional values*, that is to say those values that enable people to achieve other values, is richer. In this category we must place *life values*, *individual moral* values and *social moral* values. The first can be easily identified because they are the values connected to health. No community can neglect them. It is obvious, in fact, that being well assures full self-fulfilment and a greater performance of functional values. These life values depend upon, and assure, *individual moral* values. A citizen has the duty not to damage his health by resorting, for example, to practices such as alcoholism, drugs or others because, in doing this, he becomes a burden on the community. We should not forget that the resources that are available to secure the common good are always limited and they could be allocated to other goals, if everybody understood the importance of *individual moral* values.

These are the premiss of *social moral values*. Their gamut is notably vast but all of them work to assure that public peace and calm that is the real pre-condition for an ordered social development. Amongst them, we may remember *public morality* as well as *security* and *legal certainty*. These, in their turn, bring about justice and fairness in the difficult relationship between equality and freedom. These last two values, to be able to coexist, can never be absolutised because this leads to the disappearance of one to the detriment of the other. It follows from this that this difficult equilibrium must seek to achieve the coexistence of the greatest possible equality with the greatest possible freedom.

Lastly, there are the *specific values* that characterise the common good within a social context. These are the values of *competence* and *responsibility*, from which spring *social trust*. We should reflect on how many acts of trust we engage in from the morning to the evening, acts that allow the constant good outcome of social life precisely because we entrust ourselves – without having to engage constantly in verification – to the *competence* and *responsibility* of other people.

Cultural values form a part of *specific values* and these should be understood in the broadest sense possible. Culture is synonymous with life. In the etymological sense, it means growth; it is one of the crucial values of the common good, to which, indeed, more resources should be allocated. Let us not forget, however, that the availability of resources depends on the way in which the previous values are lived. Here there is no shortage of examples. These cultural values allow the understanding of a last group of values – *religious values*.

The etymological proximity of these two terms is truly remarkable. We should not forget that the root of 'culture' is also the root of 'cult'. But here the word 'religion' should be seen first of all with reference to its intrinsic meaning. Religion comes in the Italian language from 'to bind together again', 'to unite', 'to keep together'. A society that does not have founding values in common will encounter great difficulty in attaining an acceptable common good or, as I observed above, an optimal common good.

Let us not forget a very important fact. The religious question and religious values, 'sentenced to deportation by modern scientific reason', have been redeemed and issued 'with a permanent residence permit. The postmodern mind, more tolerant (since it is better aware of its own weaknesses) than...religiosity is, after all, nothing else but the intuition of the limits of what we, the humans, being humans, may do and comprehend'.[183] Certainly one cannot deny that the ambition of modern thought was 'to found a human order on earth, in which freedom and happiness prevailed, without any transcendental or supernatural supports'.[184] In my view – it may be observed in passing – the social doctrine of the Church was born specifically from this intention,[185] from the belief, that is to say, that at a social level, as well, it is preferable to pursue attainable goals rather than heavenly projects, which, indeed, only generate hells.

It should also be said that human beings 'haunted by uncertainty of postmodern-style need not preachers telling them about the weakness of man and the insufficiency of human resources. They need reassurance that they *can* do it – and a brief about *how* to do it'.[186] This means they look more for witnesses than for enchanters and confidence tricksters. One thus understands why it is precisely the champions of the liquid society who are forced to admit that 'One is able to act, to pursue one's own goals, to give meaning to life, if one has these relationships, these ties';[187] in essential terms: if this witness is provided.

---

183 Cf. Z. Bauman, *Postmodernity and its Discontents*, (Polity Press, Cambridge, UK – Malden, MA, USA, 1997), pp. 165, 168.

184 J. Carrol, *Humanism: the Wreck of Western Culture* (Fontana, London, 1994), p. 2.

185 Cf. R. Pezzimenti, *Perché è nata la Dottrina Sociale della Chiesa? Tra magistero e pensiero* (Soveria Mannelli, Rubbettino Editore, 2018).

186 Cf. Z. Bauman, *Postmodernity and its Discontents*, p. 179.

187 Z. Bauman, *Lo spirito e il clic. La società contemporanea fra frenesia e bisogno di speranza*, p. 28.

X. THE RISE, DECLINE AND RETURN OF SOVEREIGNTY: THE CRISIS OF GROWTH

Although it is said that sovereignty is a concept connected with the birth of the modern State, in reality it can be found in the thought and practice of the late Roman Empire. It is striking that many barbarian kingdoms after the fall of the Roman Empire created 'a normative system of two levels'. On the one hand, laws 'for the Roman population'; on the other, laws for the barbarian peoples. Certainly the criterion of sovereignty as we understand it today seems not to have had one of its *fundamental requirements*, that of exclusivity, but it is singular that there remained a 'sort of subordination at the level of ideas' as regards sovereignty understood in juridical terms by Roman law that would continue to survive in future centuries.[188] One need only think of the observations of Dante, which from many points of view were more modern than is thought, to have an idea of this.

1. Prior intimations of the question

The unity of the Roman world fascinated the architects of Germanisation. This explains why for a very long time the attempts to achieve independence of the 'national kings' were not completely successful. The barbaric populations acknowledged that the Roman Empire had that 'universality' within which the emergent nations had to locate themselves.

---

188 E. Cortese, 'Sovranità (storia)', in *Enciclopedia del Diritto*, vol. XLIII (Giuffrè Editore, Milan), 1990, p. 206.

The fact that subsequently emphasis was placed for a long time on a dual system of laws constituted 'the most accurate mirror of sovereignty and its dual value'. This was an *element* that I would say takes us back to that situation of crisis, and it perhaps enables us to understand why what we call today a crisis of sovereignty *is probably a crisis of growth*.

So-termed 'dual value' sovereignty is also the consequence of a political approach that has been at times forgotten, but which, instead, highlighted how the barbarian populations continued to see themselves, after a certain fashion, 'to a certain extent the armed arm of Rome'. Rome, that is to say, continued to be seen as the real holder of a certain sovereignty. This was something of more than a mere political nature. With the passing of the centuries, thanks to Christianity, 'it became coloured with moral tints'. The simple idea of 'subjection appeared insufficient and ties of *fidelitas* were preferred' that, with time, became increasingly personal. In this way, the elaboration took place of the principle of *rex in regno suo est imperator* which, after a certain fashion, was the pre-condition of modern absolutism.[189] The fact remains, however, that for the whole of the Middle Ages a lacerating debate persisted between those enunciations that inclined towards absolutism and those, instead, that wanted to anchor the principle of command and sovereignty in the domain of a *clear legality*.

The idea of a sovereignty not conceived in terms of absolutism is easily understandable if one takes into account that the idea of Empire that was then in force[190] – following

---

189 Cf. *ibid.*, pp. 207ff.

190 Cf. amongst many studies on the subject J. Bryce, 'Flexible and Rigid Constitutions', in *Studies in History and Jurisprudence*, vol. I (Clarendon Press, Oxford, 1901), pp. 145-252. The author examines the Roman Empire and the British Empire and highlights the special features that differentiate them from other empires. I would also like to refer here to my friend Davide Nardoni who has devoted numerous and very original studies to this subject, in particular D. Nardoni,

that of the Romans – was rather different from what we now understand it to be and from which we derive the idea of imperialism.[191] For that matter, medieval man, remembering Ulpian, knew that the power of a prince 'derived from the usual *lex regia* by which the people had transferred all power to him', thereby in factual terms limiting his action in many fields. To this should be added the fact that he could certainly not divest himself of divine law, natural law 'and by the canons of logic of the *ius gentium*'.[192] One thus understands why the variegated theories of 'resistance', which clearly anticipated a series of limitations on sovereignty, were drawn up.

Universal *sovereignty* seems for a long time to have been determined by the principles of *urgens necessitas* or even of *publica utilitas*. It seemed, that is to say, an objective fact, the source of a universal *rationabilitas*.[193] I do not believe that the reasons for this belief are of secondary importance, suggested as they were by an uncertainty due to forms of recurrent political instability caused by the perennially new invasions that, for centuries, threatened Europe. One should also add to this the fragmentation of the unity of the Mediterranean due to threats of Islamic invasion. Perhaps today, after the elapse of a long time, it is not easy to understand the atmosphere of insecurity very easily felt at that epoch.

When the situation on the Continent seemed to have stabilised, it was local situations that began to emerge as critical with recurrent internecine struggles between local lords. The objective fact of universal sovereignty 'seemed to gradually give way to the subjective fact…to the political

---

'Imperium sine fine dedi', in *Catachanna* (Accademia Italiana di Scienze Biologiche e Morali, Rome, 1979), pp. 50-64.

191 Cf. on this point R. Pezzimenti, *The Open Society and its Friends, with Letters from Isaiah Berlin and Karl R. Popper*, esp. chap. XI.

192 Cf. E. Cortese, 'Sovranità (storia)', p. 214.

193 Cf. *ibid.*, p. 219.

advance of absolutisms' of a national character that were steadily emerging. The loss of the very idea of a *universal* sovereignty meant the abandonment of its own *rationabilitas* which was being replaced by a sovereignty based upon the will of the strongest, justified on each occasion by the most disparate clauses held to be incumbent, even if exceptional. 'The overall anti-egalitarian value of these declining clauses is revealed above all else by the fact that they all occurred within the subjective world of the monarch'.[194] This explains why, in essential terms, Machiavellianism formed the basis of modern sovereignty, even if innumerable attempts took place to camouflage this.

That this idea of sovereignty was seen by many – even then – as arbitrary is indicated by the Monarchomachs. Remaining faithful to the doctrine of the popular origins of sovereignty, they continued to argue in favour of the right to resist a sovereign who had become a tyrant, even theorising his deposition and, where this was not sufficient, his elimination.[195] The positions of the Monarchomachs were present throughout Europe and this confirms not only that anti-tyranny theses had never been abandoned but also, and above all else, that they were ready to legitimise the right to resistance and revolt derived from 'social contract' positions that would be the foundation of modern constitutional theories. All of this would also be possible thanks to the recovery of that *pactum societatis* sidelined in favour of the *pactum subjectionis*: these were pacts that were subsequently brought together by Hobbes to justify absolutism and hinder every weapon of rebellion.

---

194 Cf. *ibid.*, pp. 219-220.

195 Cf. on this subject, amongst other authors, M. D'Addio, *L'idea del contratto sociale dai sofisti a Mario Salomonio* (Giuffrè Editore, Milan, 1954); L. Gambino, *Il De Republica di Pierre Grégoire. Ordine politico e monarchia nella Francia di fine Cinquecento* (Giuffrè Editore, Milan, 1978).

This was the period when the *plenitudo potestatis* of the emperor was attributed to the king who exercised it over feudal lords and subordinated cities. In essential terms, Bodin was not the innovator that many believe he was but only the man who observed and justified a phenomenon that had been underway for some time. Between this French theoretician and Hobbes there was, *inter alia*, the Thirty Years' War. With 'the Treaties of Westphalia there was a juridical recognition – however *super partes* it may have been – of the reality of the plurality of States, all in a position of equality' and all endowed with equal sovereignty. Shortly afterwards Hobbes argued that sovereign power should be a fundamental attribute of the State, which possessed it as a unity,[196] without it being shared with other powers.

In this way, the State came to acquire functions that belonged to it in a pre-eminent way. Only the State could arrange an armed intervention because war, in essential terms, was a matter between States. The people could not have a say in the question because it was considered an element peculiar to the State. With time, however, a new debate opened up that was designed to demonstrate that sovereignty belonged to the people alone or to the nation and that certain choices could be imposed.

2. The debate during modernity and the distortions of absolutism

Hayek[197] summarised a rather widespread belief in Western culture, namely that legislative activity, which finds its precondition in the concept of sovereignty, reappeared at a certain point in the Middle Ages with the 'rediscovery of Roman law'

---

196 M. S. Giannini, 'Sovranità (diritto vigente)', in *Enciclopedia del Diritto*, vol. XLIII, pp. 225-226.

197 Cf. F. A. Von Hayek, *Law Legislation and Liberty*, volume 1, *Rules and Order* (The University of Chicago, Chicago, 1973), p. 166, note 25.

and found its completion, but in my view also its distortion,[198] in modern absolutism. During that period, in fact, the idea of sovereignty derived from a precise belief: the existence of a supreme legislator whose power could not be limited; as a consequence everything that this legislator established was law because it expressed his will. Unfortunately this absolute power – typical of monarchies – was later acquired by certain democratic assemblies.[199] The concept of sovereignty thus became 'closely connected to that of political power'.[200] The effect, in truth, was to denature the very notion of law which, whereas it had been understood beforehand as a limit for power itself, was then transformed into its instrument.

As Hobbes asserted in a peremptory way, although Bacon had already expressed conclusions that were not in the least different, it was no longer truth but authority that made law. For this reason, law 'in generall, is not Counsell, but Command' and not the command of any man but only the command of he who 'is *Persona Civitatis, the Person of the Commonwealth*'.[201] This means, as John Austin argued, that the rights and duties of people, and more specifically of political subjects, depended on a single author: the Sovereign State.[202] We should reflect on the fact that despite the warning

---

198 Cf. on this subject my *The Open Society and its Friends, with Letters from Isaiah Berlin and Karl R. Popper* and *The Open Society along the Arduous Path of Modernity, with Letters from Isaiah Berlin and Hilary Putnam*.

199 Cf. F. A. Von Hayek, *Law Legislation and Liberty*, volume 1, *Rules and Order*, p. 91.

200 N. Matteucci, *Lo Stato moderno. Lessico e percorsi*, p. 81.

201 T. Hobbes, *Leviathan* (London, Penguin Books, 1980), chap. 6, p. 312.

202 The quotation from John Austin, taken from *Lectures on Jurisprudence*, is to be found in F. A. Von Hayek, *Law Legislation and Liberty*, volume 2, *The Mirage of Social Justice* (The University of Chicago, Chicago, Phoenix edition, 1978), p. 168, note 36.

of Hobbes, *non veritas sed auctoritas facit legem*, the State would tend, in the long-term, to be the real interpreter of truth. Who interprets this truth? The answer of Hobbes led to a personalisation of power in the sense that truth and authority were expressed by the sovereign, around whom revolved the person-State – Leviathan.[203] In this way States, in their relations, offered again that climate of insecurity which, *within*, was overcome by creating an authority to which everyone submits, but which, *without*, could only offer again the *bellum omnium*, given that it did not have an *auctoritas* that was recognised and obeyed by everyone.

The relationship between States was 'openly transformed into a relationship of otherness, of negation and of domination'. This was seen above all during colonial expansion when, differently from what was argued by the school of Salamanca, 'the figure of the *savage* came to be identified with that of the *alien*, who was most of the time an enemy'.[204] In truth, such a conception of sovereignty can be detected much earlier, indeed during the thirteenth century, when Beaumanoir argued that the king has supremacy over all jurisdictions and all people and that while every baron is *sovereign* in his own barony, the king is sovereign over everyone, attends to the whole of the kingdom and can therefore make *établissements* that are binding everywhere.[205] These are statements that

---

203 The Leviathan State, with its claims to truth like those of the Soviet State, are to be found in the contemporary world as well: cf. the final chapter of J. J. Chevallier, *Les grandes oeuvres politiques. De Machiavel à nos jours* (Librairie Armand Colin, Paris, 1966).

204 L. Ferrajoli, *La sovranità nel mondo moderno* (Editori Laterza, Roma-Bari, 1997), p. 26.

205 Cf. R. W. – A. J. Carlyle, *A History of Mediaeval Political Theory in the West*, vol. II, 3rd Impression (W. Blackwood & Sons Ltd., Edinburgh and London, 1950); Italian edition: Sergio Cotta (ed.), *Il pensiero politico medievale*, vol. II, edited by Luigi Firpo (Editori Laterza, Bari, 1959), p. 100.

preceded – by a long period of time – those of Bodin. Anyway they *differed* from those that were then dominant and imposed on the king, *with the right of resistance*, limitations that absolutism would ignore.

Attempts were made to see differences between the vision of Bodin and that of Hobbes 'as regards the nature of sovereignty'. Whereas the former perceived its essence above all 'in the power to pass and abrogate laws', thereby giving a higher value to legislating, the latter highlighted 'the executive moment', that is to say the coercive dimension, directed towards 'imposing specific forms of conduct'. The highly criticised ideas of *plenitudo potestatis* of Egidio Romano Colonna in this way 'had been adopted by lay people to support the political power'.[206] The fact remains that in essential terms, therefore, both resolutely encouraged and justified absolutism.

If this was the idea of *internal sovereignty*, it should be said that before this was theorised by absolutism Francisco de Vitoria formulated the idea of *external sovereignty*, which today, in the presence of the crisis of the idea of sovereignty, is of great contemporary relevance. It is truly curious that this dimension of sovereignty, 'beyond frontiers', was not taken into consideration by the fathers of the modern State. It almost seems as if disorder, which is combatted from within, was distanced and placed on the margins, confined beyond limits of security. This was not the case with Vitoria who in his famous *Relectiones* contested the *ius inventionis* invoked by the conquistadors which, beyond anything else, appeared to be in contrast with Holy Scripture. This thinker theorised three fundamental points.[207] *First*: the idea of a global order as a natural society of sovereign States, which prefigured

---

206 N. Matteucci, *Lo Stato moderno. Lessico e percorsi*, pp. 83 and 85.

207 My summary is based on L. Ferrajoli, *La sovranità nel mondo moderno*, pp. 12ff.

Francisco Suarez and the *ius gentium* later argued by Gentili and by Grotius. The individual States and their sovereigns were not for Vitoria *legibus solutus*: they were subject to laws because the law of peoples binds individual States. What was posited, therefore, was a *universalis respublica* of peoples.

Second: this idea of *external sovereignty* was 'identified with a set of natural rights of people' and ended up by establishing the bases of future international law and as Ferrajoli, paraphrasing Gaius, observes by 'substituting *homines* with *gentes*', and then defining '*quod naturalis ratio inter omnes gentes constituit, vocatur ius gentium*'.

Third: hence the consequence, still not fully resolved, that in the absence of a judge with the task of resolving certain controversies between States resort can be made to the so-termed 'just war', the only way of dealing with *iniuriae*.

However, the fact remains important that such *external sovereignty* remained anchored in natural law. The same could not be said about internal sovereignty which, once made autonomous from natural law, as from morality and theology, led to law and sovereignty itself being justified by facts, or to put it better, by the interests and the *will* of politics.[208]

Why did this absurdity come about? Popper's view was that modern thought about sovereignty, starting from the idea of understanding in whom it resides, posed itself a single question: *who should govern?* Questions of this kind involve rather dangerous answers such as: the wise, the governor by birth, the general will, the superior race, the proletariat, the people, etc. These are all answers that set aside more serious and legitimate questions which in essential terms depended on a crucial question: *how can we organise political institutions in a way that impedes bad*

---

208 Cf. *ibid.*, p. 21. This is also one of the strong points of Rosmini's *Filosofia del diritto*.

or incompetent governors from doing too much damage? However, in answering the question 'who should rule', we gave rise to what for Popper is the 'theory of (unchecked) sovereignty'.[209] This is a theory that went from Bodin to Hegel, passing by way of Rousseau.

3. The contemporary situation

What all absolutist writers and those who depend upon them, such as Marx and Hegel, have in common is an earthly dream of an 'earthly paradise' that is not meta-historical, a 'brave new world', to cite Popper, that is able to transform human beings themselves. The gross error of such theories about sovereignty is that they remove any sense of limits, any theory of 'checks and balances'. In this way, a simple fact is forgotten: 'governments are not always good or wise',[210] and the roots of this uncertainty cannot be extirpated once and for all. Thus was posited, as was done by many and by Rousseau himself, a sort of original sin that altered human nature, as well as the natural criterion of equality, and which, whatever the case, can be easily removed.[211] The man from Geneva, when we understand things correctly, when speaking about sovereignty went beyond the idea of a 'substantial reality'. The general will, in being opposed to particular wills, abandons all utilitarian criteria and confers upon sovereignty a rigorous 'moral' value.[212] The criterion

---

209 Cf. K. R. Popper, *The Open Society and its Enemies*, vol. I, *The Spell of Plato*, p. 121.

210 *Ibid.*, p. 122.

211 Cf. on this subject my *Politica e Religione. La secolarizzazione nella modernità* (Città Nuova Editrice, Rome, 2004), translated into Spanish with an introduction by J. Y. Calvez, *Política y religión. Legado cultural de la secularización* (Ciudad Nueva, Buenos Aires, 2008).

212 Cf. N. Matteucci, *Lo Stato moderno. Lessico e percorsi*, p. 89.

of sovereignty became an almost religious concept, albeit of an earthly religion. Rousseau was led to invent the 'general will', a sort of 'super-personality', to which he gave the characteristics of infallibility, indivisibility, inalienability, absoluteness, etc. These characteristics were gradually acquired by a race and then by a class that grew 'as orthodox Christianity declined, replacing the latter with belief in a mystical experience of its own'.[213] The idea of sovereignty, in Popper's view, became in Hegel a nationalism that was 'a well-disciplined Prussian authoritarianism', in the same way, it should be added, as class was disciplined in the party. Here Popper is of the view that Hegel's thoughts on English institutions 'are ridiculous', given that to him they even seemed backward. The fact is that to what was being defined as the 'minimal state' he opposed the 'almighty state'.[214] However, this had before it not interlocutors but adversaries.

Lacking a 'pre-established sovereign reality', we have before us an anarchic international society. This anarchy is expressed in 'an indeterminate power, intolerant of restrictions, unconcerned about boundaries, and determined to develop the capacity to impose its own will'. It is for this reason in some people's view that 'hyper-States' are becoming established that have a

---

213 Cf. K. R. Popper, *The Open Society and its Enemies*, vol. II, *The High Tide of Prophecy Hegel and Marx* (Routledge & Kegan Paul, London, 1974), pp. 52 and 55. The second quotation is in reality from E. N. Anderson.

214 *Ibid.*, pp. 56ff. It is very interesting that Popper does not see Christianity as responsible for this absurdity of modernity: 'The medieval conversion of Christianity into an authoritarian creed could not fully suppress its humanitarian tendencies; again and again, Christianity breaks through the authoritarian cloak (and is persecuted as heresy)': *ibid.*, p. 58.

propensity to exercise 'the projection of power abroad'.[215] This is a will that is expressed today in an abused analysis of globalisation that was theorised, and I would say hoped for, by Marx himself,[216] and which brings about as a reaction phenomena involving the search for identity that are often exaggerated.

To return to the *theory of unchecked sovereignty*, it should be said that this is the salient feature of totalitarian democracies that do not have any 'institutional control of the rulers by the ruled'. Popper thus argued, and in a way that for some was bizarre, that *all theories of sovereignty are paradoxical*, in the sense that no sovereignty can see itself as absolute. For this reason, every 'theory of sovereignty is in a weak position, both empirically and logically'.[217]

This belief became established thanks to those theories that tried to reduce the absolutist claims of sovereignty. Where this involved the power to make the final decision, a turning point was sought with the French Revolution which identified the people as the subject that possesses 'incontestably the right to determine the operational framework and legal and political rules in a specific territory'. Taking up the classic distinction between *formal* and *substantial* sovereignty, in effect on the people is bestowed the former given that 'who actually exercises it [substantial sovereignty] are its representatives'. It has been rightly observed that this popular sovereignty 'opens

---

215 P. Ferrare, 'Prospettive per una democrazia post-sovranista', in *Sofia. Ricerche sui fondamenti e la correlazione dei saperi, Rivista semestrale*, Anno III, n. 1, 2001, p. 51.

216 On this subject see R. Pezzimenti, 'Globalizzazione: natura, vantaggi e contraddizioni', in F. Compagnoni and A. Lo Presti (eds.), *Etica e globalizzazione* (Città Nuova Editrice, Rome, 2006), pp. 35ff.

217 Cf. K. R. Popper, *The Open Society and its Enemies*, vol. I, *The Spell of Plato*, pp. 123-124.

up the road to secularisation'[218] or, to put it another way, to a different way of seeing the common good. This sovereignty based on representation, before being a political institution 'is a sociological fact of great importance for the development of modernity', even if it can run the risk of 'being denatured into autocracy' by by-passing popular sovereignty. It is for this reason that 'forms of direct democracy' were subsequently envisaged 'such as *referendums* or *legislative measures proposed by the public*', specifically in order to allow the people to intervene when their sovereignty was really threatened'.[219] From this arose the liberal doctrine of the rule of law which is nothing else than a delineation of powers and in a certain sense of sovereignty itself. For this reason, I do not feel that I can agree with those who argue that to establish limits to 'its activity means a doctrine that denies sovereignty'.[220] Sovereignty *followed the evolution of the State* and underwent the same limitation of powers. When this did not take place there was a fall either into the general will of Rousseau or even worse into the 'ethical State' of Hegel, which meant that the *temptation of absolute sovereignty* has continued until today, and, masked in various ways, I believe it continues to survive even today when the omnipotence of the legislative power is invoked.

As regards Hegel, the omnipotence of the State became the omnipotence of its sovereignty which encountered neither internal nor external limits. Hence *on the one hand* the right of the State to wage war for the rational (but not necessarily reasonable) pursuit of its national

---

218 C. Mongardini, *Pensare la politica. Per una analisi critica della politica contemporanea* (Bulzoni Editore, Rome, 2011), pp. 117-119.

219 Cf. *ibid.*, p. 120.

220 L. Ferrajoli, *La sovranità nel mondo moderno*, p. 30.

interests, and *on the other* its absolute internal autonomy with full control over the population, and obviously over minorities, and, as a consequence, over resources and the national territory.[221] Individuals and things are at the mercy of every decision it takes.

4. The foundations and limits of sovereignty

With respect to internal sovereignty, Gaetano Mosca perhaps got it right when he spoke about two principles – the aristocratic and the democratic – that are never achieved in an absolute sense. In a certainly pessimistic way, not least because of the period he lived in, Mosca came to argue that democracies could enter into difficulty because of 'the monopoly of violence held by the State'; violence that in the view of Ferrero allowed a 'mobilisation of popular consent'. Aside from these considerations, the fact remains that the formula of a 'mixed government' envisaged by Mosca 'characterises modern sovereignty with a changing barycentre'.[222] It is for this reason that some scholars[223] speak about incomplete democracy or even of a sovereign people that cannot be found.

All of this complicates the problem at its roots. Indeed, there has not been sufficient reflection on the factor that

---

221 Cf. J. Rawls, *Lectures on the History of Moral Philosophy*, by the President and Fellows of Harvard College, 2000, 'Hegel', chap. II, 3.

222 C. Mongardini, *Pensare la politica. Per una analisi critica della politica contemporanea*, p. 120. Mongardini refers to the inaugural lecture of 1902 given by Gaetano Mosca at the University of Turin: *Principio aristocratico e democratico nel passato e nell'avvenire*.

223 Cf. P. Rosanvillon *Le people introuvable. Histoire de la représentation démocratique en France* (Éditions du Seuil, Paris, 1998); *La démocratie inachevée. Histoire de la représentation démocratique en France* (Éditions du Seuil, Paris, 2000).

continues to differentiate individual States and to divide them on the increasingly complex possibility of finding a shared foundation on which to begin to speak about shared sovereignty, a foundation that enables us to address the subject of the limits to sovereignty as well.

This foundation in the view of one of the first modern liberals, David Hume, is conventional wisdom. To carry this concept to extremes and to follow Hayek we have in front of us a serious problem because if every power is based upon public opinion this principle is more 'true... of an absolute dictator than those of any other authority'. Indeed, it is no accident that all dictators 'are so concerned to manipulate opinion through their control of information which is in their power'.[224] For this reason, and not always with the hoped for success, an attempt was made to apply brakes to sovereignty.

For a certain period it was thought that such a limit could come from the established and recognised foundations on which sovereignty was founded. This was one of the assumptions of legal positivism itself. One should remember that this term derives from the Latin '*positus*', designed, hence '*positivus*', to emphasise 'the deliberate creation of all law by human will',[225] which on its own can place – indeed has placed, *positus* – limits on the faculty to legislate. Thus the will to legislate – sovereignty – depends on what the will of citizens sees as just. Yet this concept is also exposed to possible forms of degeneration of democracy that can precipitate either into authoritarianism or into co-called totalitarian democracy. Indeed, this has been one of the most dangerous outcomes of the positivist

---

[224] Cf. F. A. Vov Hayek, *Law Legislation and Liberty*, vol. 1, *Rules and Order*, p. 92.

[225] F. A. Von Hayek, *Law Legislation and Liberty*, volume 2, *The Mirage of Social Justice*, p. 45.

idea of sovereignty.[226] This is an idea of democracy and thus of sovereignty that today is rather fashionable. According to this theory, no restrictions of any kind can be placed on sovereignty. This is almost a return to the concept of Renaissance sovereignty which was gradually eroded specifically because limits were placed on it.

'The pretended logical necessity of such an unlimited source of power simply does not exist' in the people. In addition, more than asking who possesses or has a right to exercise a specific power, one should ask 'whether the exercise of such a power by any agency is justified by the implicit terms of submission'. This is an issue that is also rather old, indeed as old as *consensus iuris*.[227] The people, that is to say, limit a power but they cannot, because of this, manage an unlimited power. One need only think that the institution of the referendum in some Constitutions, such as the Italian Constitution, encounters precise restrictions. The same should be said – and this seems self-evident – about personal forms of sovereignty underpinned by popular consent, even if this in progressively diversified forms of populism often seems to reappear. Weber's denomination 'plebiscitary democracy' should make us reflect.

To paraphrase Rosanvallon, one may say that the people, already the holder of sovereignty, clearly lose their form and end up by being identified with a 'charisma' to which they are drawn. 'In this sense sovereignty is the personalisation of a force-idea in which are found the historical necessity, the capacity of those who hold power, and the essential

---

226 As regards the possible degenerations of democracy, Hayek observes that 'the whole history of constitutionalism, at least since John Locke, which is the same as the history of liberalism, is that of a struggle against the positivist conception of sovereignty and the allied conception of the omnipotent state': *ibid.*, p. 61.

227 F. A. Von Hayek, *Law Legislation and Liberty*, volume 3, *The Political Order of a Free People*, pp. 33-34.

conditions of a culture'.²²⁸ This is the proof that it is precisely this last that ends up by giving a soul to politics and to sovereignty itself.

This observation is fundamental because although it is true that an idea of *sovereignty* is an *idea that evolves*, it is equally true – as I have already observed – that it must ask itself on what it is based if it does not want to run the risk of being overwhelmed and dissipating the arduous achievements that have been attained. For this reason, I do not agree with the conclusion offered by Hayek, according to which 'if we asked on what sovereignty is based, the answer would be on nothing – if not temporarily on the constituent organ'.²²⁹ This is a conclusion that had a post-modern flavour when nobody thought this.

It seems to me that the conclusion of Bobbio is more thoughtful. In his view 'the fundamental problem of the theorists of sovereignty has also been that of presenting it not as naked power' but as something with a foundation, 'a power of law, that is to say a power that is also authorised and regulated, like the lower powers, by a higher norm'. It is clear that this could, in different circumstances, be of divine origins, 'a natural law or a fundamental law' based upon a constitution or tradition.²³⁰ To summarise, what counts is that its foundation was necessary.

When speaking about the foundation of the concept of sovereignty one could also start from the natural theory of justice theorised by Rawls. Moving from the assumption that a society that assures stability is a society where 'the natural duty of justice would be agreed to rather than a principle of utility', and establishing a close tie between stability and

---

228 C. Mongadini, *Pensare la politica. Per una analisi critica della politica contemporanea*, p. 124.

229 *Ibid.*, p. 123.

230 N. Bobbio, *Teoria generale della politica*, p. 185.

sovereignty, one can say that the latter cannot be founded only on strictly empirical rules. Indeed, the natural duty of justice begins 'with the duty of mutual respect...This is the duty to show a person the respect which is due him as a moral being, that is, as a being with a sense of justice and a conception of the good'.[231] This confirms, as I will observe shortly, that the idea of law, and as a consequence of sovereignty, is an idea based upon meta-empirical concepts of justice.

It should also be said that if indeed a close tie exists between stability and sovereignty then this leads to a crisis of the idea of sovereignty of Carl Schmitt. He argues that 'sovereign is he who decides on when there is an exceptional circumstance since this circumstance can be decided on only by who...can in the end take a decision without being authorised by someone above him'.[232] Yet this is in contrast with the idea of sovereignty that has just been referred to because sovereignty was born, and above all developed, specifically to move out of exceptionality and precariousness in order to live in stability and in 'certainty'.

In addition, to accept the position of Schmitt makes us 'defenders of arbitrary sovereignty; the law is the whim of the strongest'. These defenders propose anew – perhaps without wanting to – absolute sovereignty, because law becomes the justifiable command of the strongest. The difference, at least from a substantial point of view, becomes notably small if this 'strongest' is the 'economically dominant class (Marx)' or if, as Mosca affirmed, it is the political class, or according to Mills the 'power elite' or any other social group. What matters is that all are 'able to decide on an exceptional circumstance', [233] as Schmitt himself wanted.

---

231 J. Rawls, *A Theory of Justice* (Oxford University Press, Oxford, 1989), p. 337.

232 N. Bobbio, *Teoria generale della politica*, p. 419.

233 Cf. N. Matteucci, *Lo Stato moderno. Lessico e percorsi*, pp. 89-90.

At this point sovereignty could appear 'a sleeping power' that is able to reveal itself only at particular moments when social cohesion fades or when ideas of sovereignty irrupt that are alternatives to the idea in force. In this case, sovereignty is seen solely as the possibility of 'creating' a new order before going back 'into hibernation'.[234] This is a decidedly restrictive approach.

5. The rights of the person and other limits for sovereignty

From what has just been said, it follows that if sovereignty was born to assure a sense of civic and social order within a specific territory then 'a society regulated by a public sense of justice is inherently stable'. It is obvious that this idea of justice cannot be a simple and abstract assertion because the 'most stable conception of justice...is presumably one that is perspicuous to our reason'.[235] It is specifically reason, underpinned by concrete experience, that enables us to understand that the above-mentioned criteria of justice can – and are – constantly threatened. 'So even in a just society it is reasonable to admit certain constraining arrangements to insure compliance, but their main purpose is to underwrite citizen's trust in one another'.[236] Security and mutual trust take us back to the original pre-conditions of sovereignty but here they are seen anew in a different light.

To all of this another observation should be added: the emergence of new supranational realities that have led us to see the 'subjects of international law as no longer only States but also individuals and peoples'. We may think of the right to self-determination which generated an innovation comparable at an internal level to that of the

---

234 Cf. *ibid.*, p. 93.

235 J. Rawls, *A Theory of Justice*, pp. 498-499.

236 *Ibid.*, p. 577.

establishment of administrative justice during the second part of the nineteenth century, before which 'an appeal of a citizen against the State before state jurisdictions would have been inconceivable'.[237] All of this demonstrates that *sovereignty* is a concept *in fieri*.

To create a new sovereignty, 'an effective limitation of the sovereignty of States' is not enough: we also need to recognise individuals and peoples as effective subjects of law. When it comes to the rights of peoples, Vitoria still has something to suggest to us. His contemporary relevance is emphasised when he speaks to us about *ius societatis et communicationis* or, even more, about *ius peregrinandi* and *ius migrandi*, which he holds to be natural rights and a 'universalistic paradigm of fundamental rights',[238] which, alas, are too often ignored. As regards *ius peregrinandi* and *ius migrandi*, it should be said that these highlight how today we live in 'an epoch of increasing *heteronomy*' that is characterised by governments that 'are no longer the exclusive actors of international politics', demonstrating once again how sovereignty 'must by now take into account global governance'.[239] In this contingency, it is in fact the rights of individuals that are infringed and frequently even more than the rights of peoples.

A consideration of the rights of individuals is required given that these could constitute the true foundation of a new way of understanding sovereignty. We could start from Rosmini for whom the Hegelian idea of 'domination is repugnant to the deep nature of man'. Man, for Rosmini, has rights that are not won – they descend from his very being as a person. The person, indeed, is a 'subsistent right'. 'It is not that man has a right to his own personhood: in

---

237 L. Ferrajoli, *La sovranità nel mondo moderno*, p. 41.

238 Cf. *ibid.*, pp. 52, 54.

239 P. Ferrara, 'Prospettive per una democrazia post-sovranista', pp. 50-51.

that case two persons would be distinguished in man, one having rights, the other being the subject of rights. On the contrary the one having rights is the person himself who is the subject of rights'.[240] This observation emphasises the deep sensitivity of Rosmini who is concerned about all the difficulties that any person could encounter. This is because 'a right exists whenever there exists a person, who is destined at least to suffer, in which case in other persons there exists a moral duty not to be the cause of his pain'.[241] From this derives an immediate coextension of rights and the person

Every idea of sovereignty, therefore, cannot be separated from this juridical foundation if it really wants to respect individuals. From this it follows that the essence is not 'legislation and the law but the person – in his structural *relational nature*'.[242] This relational nature is extremely important because, on the one hand, it *emphasises* the dynamism that is typical of every person and, on the other, it criticises the belief that rights derive solely from the State.

Here Rosmini goes well beyond Kant. Rights, being generated by the person, relate not only to exteriority but to the whole of the human being. Respect for the other arises from interiority. 'If, therefore, the person is supreme activity by his nature, it is manifest to him that one must find in other persons the corresponding moral duty not to injure him, not even to think of this, an attempt directed to offending him or subordinating him, depriving him of his natural supremacy, as one sees when applying the moral

---

240 A. Rosmini, *Filosofia del diritto (1841-1843)*, vol. I, edited by R. Orecchia (CEDAM, Padua, 1967), n. 48, p. 191.

241 *Ibid.*, n. 43, p. 190. G. Campanini,

242 G. Campanini, *Politica e società in Antonio Rosmini* (Editrice A. V. E., Rome, 1997), pp. 36-37.

principle we established of *recognising practically things for what they are*.[243] All of this means that whoever exercises sovereignty and society itself must respect the same laws that every individual must respect.

Nor does this mean that a human being acquires more strength by living in a social context. This is because 'the individual person, in becoming a part of the social person, only acquires a further relationship and does not destroy himself'.[244] This also means that the respect due to a person does not depend on the social context in which he finds himself. 'Rights in a person, the corresponding obligation to respect them in others, after a certain fashion place a division between persons'.[245] Here lies that limit that not even 'universal social law' can transgress.

It is certainly no accident that for Rosmini law must be the foundation of politics and this to the point that political philosophy can begin where the bases of the philosophy of law have been established. This means that justice cannot be only the purpose of politics – it must be its precondition.[246] It is from here that today all thought must begin about sovereignty which, to paraphrase Pascal, is connected with the *infinitely small*, the individual person, and the *infinitely large*, that is to say world society at risk, as Ulrich Beck would say. Indeed, if, on the one hand, the rights of the most forgotten about of the globe must be defended, the 'dangers that humanity has to address today (climate change, transnational terrorism, world financial crises, food and health-care emergencies on a planetary

---

243 A. Rosmini, *Filosofia del diritto (1841-1843)*, vol. I, n. 52, p. 192.

244 A. Rosmini, *Filosofia del diritto (1841-1843)*, vol. III, edited by R. Orecchia (CEDAM, Padua, 1969), n. 1649, p. 600.

245 *Ibid.*, n. 27, p. 723.

246 A. Rosmini, *Filosofia del diritto (1841-1843)*, vol. VI, edited by R. Orecchia (CEDAM, Padua, 1969), nn. 2578ff, pp. 1579ff.

scale)' create 'a sort of *forced cosmopolitanism*'.[247] These are international choices that at times are more experienced than decided.

There is the real danger that an anti-democratic sovereignty will be established. Not only forms of fundamentalism but also, and above all else, populism, self-justified by efficiency, require the greatest attention. All of this could renew dangerous positions of international hegemony that would be able to bring back sovereignty to an absolutist realm that is distant from democratic pre-conditions. Wolin speaks about democracy managed by the other or, even better, of the smiling face of overturned totalitarianism. From this starts the idea of 'responsible sovereignty' defined as an 'invitation to moderation' which should be addressed above all to those who, specifically at an international level, 'have for long practised irresponsible sovereignty, that is to say in a unilateral way',[248] showing that they are insensitive to what has happened to the rest of humanity.

This means that a new concept of sovereignty can temper the possible extreme forms of globalisation, as well as the growing subjection of internal legal systems to international ones, defending a 'greater establishment of forms of local autonomy'. These last, amongst other things, can compensate for 'the breakdown of the hierarchical order of bourgeois society under the pressure in a horizontal sense of social powers'. In this case, reference has been made to *negotiated sovereignty*, that is to say sovereignty 'without unquestioned predominance'.[249] This would seem

---

247 P. Ferrara, 'Prospettive per una democrazia post-sovranista', p. 55. The book by Ulrich Beck to which reference is made in the Italian edition is *Il Dio personale* (Editori Laterza, Rome-Bari, 2009).

248 Cf. *ibid.*, p. 52.

249 C. Mongardini, *Pensare la politica. Per una analisi critica della politica contemporanea*, p. 125.

to validate the thesis of those who speak about a crisis of sovereignty.

6. Can one really speak about a crisis of sovereignty?

To speak about a crisis or eclipse[250] of sovereignty can be suggestive and dangerous. It was already talked about when civil society returned to playing a determining role thanks to parties, or when trade unions developed and gave new lymph to intermediate bodies or, lastly, when the rise of a philosophy of companies created a new vision for local autonomies which were no longer, and not only, of a political or administrative nature but also of an economic and financial character.

One could then 'commit the same mistake that was made with the thesis of *the end of ideologies* or *the end of history*'. The end of a 'type of ideology' does not mean the end of all ideologies. The same could take place when speaking about the sovereignty of the State. Indeed, one cannot forget that 'sovereignty is deliberately negotiated with institutions and forces that owe their existence and their capacity for imposition to the State'.[251] That is to say the State and its sovereignty are perhaps becoming weaker but certainly being transformed. Here an essential element of sovereignty is probably absent. We should remember that it is based upon an assumption that was subject to in-depth examination as early as the Middle Ages: the principle of command and the principle of sovereignty must be exercised within a context of evident legality. This simple observation leads us to go beyond the aspects of the current crisis of sovereignty. Indeed, 'if sovereignty is the sum of supreme powers....

---

250 Cf. N. Matteucci, *Lo Stato moderno. Lessico e percorsi*, pp. 97ff.

251 C. Mongardini, *Pensare la politica. Per una analisi critica della politica contemporanea*, p. 127.

legally unlimited powers do not exist'.[252] It is the obsolete conception of absolute sovereignty, which for that matter was also criticised at its moment of greatest splendour, that is in crisis. Starting from this assumption, the crisis of sovereignty can be defined as a *crisis of growth* towards forms that are necessarily new and more useful in relation to the new questions and issues that have to be addressed. This is why I believe that we should agree with the thesis of those who argue that if we are to speak about a crisis or an eclipse of sovereignty 'this phenomenon should certainly be referred to the instrumental use that twentieth century thought, in particular publicly debated legal thought, made of that category'. It should remembered that 'theoretical discourse about sovereignty always remains levelled to the doctrine of political realism',[253] and this makes us forget that, as is the case of all political terms whose meaning tends to evolve, the meaning of sovereignty, too, is undergoing a radical transformation.

Lastly, to level down the doctrine of political realism means to reduce sovereignty to a mere fact of emergency, giving it 'a legitimation of a Hobbesian type'.[254] Even starting from here, however, one can retrieve some cardinal features of sovereignty that, ever since a sense of law has been present in society, has constituted one of the cardinal features of civil life. Indeed, how can we forget that sovereignty 'arose together *with a sense of limit'?* From this springs a sense of the *legitimacy of power*, as well as a legal sense of being together in society, that is to say the

---

252 M. S. Giannini, 'Sovranità (diritto vigente)', p. 228.
253 Cf. F. M. Di Sciullo, 'Eclissi della sovranità? Voci di un dibattito (1989-2009)', in G. Giunta, (ed.), *La politica tra storia e diritto. Scritti in memoria di Luigi Gambino* (Franco Angeli, Milan, 2012), pp. 259-260.
254 Cf. *ibid.*, p. 266.

*criterion of citizenship.*²⁵⁵ Aspects such as a *sense of limit, the legitimacy of power and the criterion of citizenship* constitute fixed points of all political analysis: aspects that once again highlight that if we are to speak about a crisis, the crisis of sovereignty is a crisis of growth.

In addition, the very forgoing of portions of sovereignty should often be seen as to the advantage of other forms that assure greater security, stability and legality. When I say these things I am thinking of those European politicians who at the end of the Second World War spoke explicitly about a reduction of the sovereignty of individual States, but they did this to the advantage of a European sovereignty which today, if we look closely, everyone invokes given the international weakness of our Union.

For this reason, I believe, if one accepts this definition, that the *new concept of sovereignty* depends upon the search for a coexistence between respect for the *universal rights of man* and an *exclusive sovereignty* that has to be envisaged to address international problems such as those that have been referred to, i.e. climate change, transnational terrorism, world financial crises and food and health-care emergencies on a planetary scale. However, this is an equilibrium that can – and must – be strengthened by an increasing affirmation of local autonomies, respecting the two containers that have just been indicated.

---

255 Cf. *ibid.*, pp. 262-263.

XI. POLYARCHY. MULTICULTURAL AND MULTI-ETHNIC SOCIETIES: ADVANTAGES, DANGERS AND A SENSE OF LIMITS

One can agree, to return to a quotation of Bobbio that is frequently invoked, 'that every social group has a natural tendency to a stiffening of its structures the more the number of its members grows and the range of its activities is extended. An apparently pluralistic society is in reality polycratic, that is to say it has a number of centres of power, each one of which makes its own claims prevail over those of its individual members'.[256] This explains why such a 'polycratic' vision is contrary to every vision of statism and in general against every kind of statist monism.

It is certainly no accident that what we define today as polyarchy was formulated in the United States of America. It was there that de Tocqueville, 'without any Eurocentric prejudice', detected the origins of pluralist society which he certainly did not define as such but whose seeds he highlighted. This French thinker acted 'on the axiom that in the United States it is the people that govern, his analysis starts from society: when he speaks about institutions he dwells at length upon local autonomies...his attention is directed above all else to civil society' and all of its multiform associations. *Démocratie en Amérique*, in exalting the role of civil associations, does not only offer a critique of statism embodied by a paternalist State which

---

256 N. Bobbio, 'Pluralismo', p. 722.

provides for everything – it is also a decisive critique of that individualism that wants to close up the individual in a selfish way in his own private life.[257] This is a critique that is often forgotten about but which, instead, de Tocqueville pursues in a precise way, being worried about possible anarchic or solipsistic developments of society.

The possibility of adhering to various associations confers stability on the political system not only because it withdraws the individual from 'direct contact with the State' but also because it allows the individual to relate in a supportive way to the various groups that exist and could exist. These groups obtain strength by basing themselves on 'free association between individuals'. This observation, which is apparently a platitude, is the point of departure of MacIver. 'He observes that we live in a community prior to living in a State, that is to say we live in a delimited area of society'. The various organisations and associations arise either 'from shared economic interests' or 'from shared interests' – interests that are cultural, religious, philosophical, scientific etc. MacIver certainly did not intend to abolish the role of government within a State; it was only that 'it must not intervene in the lives of the cultural communities at work in society'. If anything, its task is to 'regulate the activity of economic associations' which, left to themselves, would run the risk of compromising the social order.[258] This position, which in my view is sound, is nothing else but the need to limit the action of the political sphere.

This position was subsequently broadened by Rawls for whom, by circumscribing the sphere of political action

---

257 Cf. N. Matteucci, 'Pluralismo', in *Enciclopedia delle scienze sociali*, www.treccani.it (consulted 13.05.2011).

258 *Ibidem*; the reference work by the American scholar is R. Maciver, *The Web of Government* (New York, 1947).

alone, it is possible to respect the real plurality of moral, philosophical and religious principles.[259] This is so-termed 'reasonable pluralism', which I prefer to call concrete pluralism[260] because its point of reference is the concrete person who acts.

To return to polyarchy, it should be said that it should no longer be seen as the only form of democracy but as one form that democracy can take. One can therefore argue 'that *democracy* and *polyarchy* indicate different things'. In addition, as Dahl points out, polyarchy is a set of institutions that are not economic but political in character. The industrial or post-industrial market economy 'is neither a necessary nor a sufficient condition for polyarchy' which, indeed, developed within the context of prevalently agricultural economic conditions. Many countries, amongst which the United States, Canada, those of the whole of Oceania, and yet others, demonstrate this fact. In opposite fashion, one can say that when the institutions of a polyarchy are sufficiently solid, they can become compatible with any economic system.[261] Polyarchy is thus any specific form of democracy and indicates processes and institutions of that type of representative democracy that developed during the twentieth century.

To be more precise, Dahl highlights certain conditions that foster polyarchy. First of all, a) the presence of a democratic culture and democratic ideas. Then, b) a real control over the army and the security forces. Followed by c) modern economic and social systems. In addition, there is d) law and order where behaviour that is arbitrary and not

---

259 Cf. J. Rawls, *Political Liberalism* (Oxford University Press, Oxford, 1993).

260 Cf. in this work chap. III.

261 Cf. R.A. Dahl, 'Poliarchia', in *Enciclopedia delle scienze sociali*, www.treccani.it (consulted 16.06.2011).

regulated by law are absent or at the most insubstantial. To these should be added e) that these requirements must find within the country in question a certain level of *homogeneity*. To conclude, f) the State where polyarchy is implemented must enjoy independence.[262] It is for this reason that one of the threats to polyarchy comes from the internationalisation of politics. A reason for tension could also be the market economy if it manages to compromise one of the salient characteristics of the polyarchic system which is provided by equality, above all when economic resources end up by being used in order to control or deform information, to the point of being a source of corruption.

1. Polyarchy and multiculturalism

To what risks is a polyarchic society based upon a widespread idea of pluralism exposed? I believe that Matteucci correctly identified the real danger that comes from so-called multicultural and multi-ethnic societies. Whereas the first cannot solely coexist, indeed their 'mutual exchange is translated into an authentic enrichment for everyone', the second can be 'closed societies, tied to the memories of their own past and with blood ties: it is kinship and not citizenship that keeps them together'.[263] This is a diversity that should be emphasised and which can be overcome only by anchoring the action of multi-ethnic societies in respect for the 'person' and his inalienable rights.

For authentic respect for the 'person' to exist, as we are reminded by Taylor, it is presumed that a tie exists between 'recognition and identity'. It is the second term

---

262 Cf. *Ibidem*. The order in which I have expressed the premises of polyarchy is slightly different from that offered by Dahl.

263 Cf. N. Matteucci, 'Pluralismo', in *Enciclopedia Italiana Treccani*.

that in multicultural societies captures the vision that a person has of his own fundamental characteristics that define him as a human being. Without these, there is a sort of non-recognition that tends, whatever the case, to cause injury. All of this means that identity cannot be constructed in isolation but is perceived and enriched by entering into dialogue with others.[264] Identity cannot be a predefined script, in the same way as no culture and no multiculturalism can be such.

The observations made hitherto, once again according to Taylor, led to the birth of the 'politics of universalism' which confers not only equality of rights but also equal dignity of rights for citizens. In addition, the modern notion of identity 'created the politics of difference'. This last, an assumption of the politics of identity, developed, starting, however, with the politics of universal dignity to which was added 'something' specific, 'which for each man is only his'.[265] We would say that it is his special aspect, a *proprius* from which he cannot be separated.

If this is the case, not only does this mean that differences cannot be homogenised but also that the alternative to multiculturalism can only be barbarity.[266] Fear of cultural dialogue impoverishes us and the very claim to defend a culture makes it barren. Ennius, at the beginning of Roman multiculturalism, could say that he possessed three souls because he spoke three languages.[267]

---

264 Cf. C. Taylor, *Multiculturalism and 'The Politics of Recognition'*, *With Commentary by* A. Gutmann, edited by, S. C. Rockefeller, M. Walzer, S. Wolf, (Princeton University Press, 1992), chap. I, pp. 25ff.

265 Cf. *ibid*, chap. II, pp. 37ff.

266 Cf. *Ibid.*, chap. V, p. 72. Taylor takes this definition from Roger Kimball.

267 Cf. R. Pezzimenti, *The Open Society and its Friends, with Letters from Isaiah Berlin and Karl R. Popper*, 1.2.

We should not forget that language is one of the most important instruments of a process of socialisation. It is only this last, in the view of Habermas,[268] that allows a person to acquire his identity. Law could remain in an abstract domain if it did not descend into the concrete of the process of integration. This explains why a person must be recognised within a community that is integrated around a specific conception of good. For this reason, one can speak about *ethical integration* which otherwise would not have meaning and one would continue to move within the vagueness of a *political integration* that at times could be abstract. Only after ethical integration does political integration have a real sense. Indeed, it becomes absolutely necessary since 'it produces loyalty towards a shared political culture'.[269] Without this real integration, multiculturalism does not manage, most of the time, to detach itself from 'multi-ethnicism'.

The position of multiculturalism, understood correctly, seems to be a position that is difficult to attack. No culture can argue that it is pure and immune to contaminations. Every 'cultural sphere rarely appears monolithic'. If we see it as such, this is because each one of us tends to consider as our own in fact what we owe to others, including strangers. 'The past tries to structure itself as a framework that tends to adapt the new in a reassuring way'. Everything that does not reassure is seen as extraneous, 'as a source of insecurity and blame and others as the origins of injustice, faithlessness and decline'. To have a

---

268 J. Habermas, *Kampfum Anerkennung im Demokratischen Rechtsstaat* (Suhrkamp Verlag, Frankfurt am Main, 1996). For the Italian edition from which these quotations are taken see C. Taylor and J. Habermas, *Multiculturalismo. Lotte per il riconoscimento*.

269 Cf. *ibid.*, §4.

positive position on the subject we would have to admit that there is 'in truth a mass of multiculturalisms'.[270] The positions of liberals and communitarians have recently addressed this subject. I will not dwell upon the question that Armellini addressed in an exhaustive way when answering the question of recognition to which, as he summarises rather effectively, 'the policies of universalism of the classical tradition, or the policies of difference proposed by communitarianism, responded'.[271] I will start from this point to address another question.

Let us bear in mind, to return to the disputation between Taylor and Habermas, that their positions have advantages and defects from the two points of view that have just been outlined. 'Liberal universalism runs the risk of being discriminatory when it denies public relevance' but the position of Habermas ends up 'by placing before procedural consensus the value of political culture adopted acritically as such and not presented as a problem'.[272] The two above-mentioned thinkers 'do not solve the central problem of modern political thought that makes the State a space of security which leaves outside

---

270 P. Armellini, 'Il dibattito sul multiculturalismo in Nord America', in M. P. Paternò (ed.), *Noi e gli altri, ipotesi di inclusione nel dibattito contemporaneo* (Rubbettino Editore, Soveria Mannelli, Catanzaro, 2008), pp. 30-31.

271 *Ibid.*, p. 35. As regards the communitarians, Armellini wrote: 'For this reason they formulate a conception of rationality in which is privileged the role of reflection, deliberation and the assessment of norms and values and a conception of the subject agent that locates him in a historical and social context. In addition, for them there exists a constitutive role of the ends and the values of the community that is belonged to for the political and moral identity of individuals' (*ibidem*).

272 *Ibid.*, pp. 35 and 39. Of interest here are the observations of Armellini on the distinction between political liberalism and metaphysical liberalism.

what is beyond its boundaries, that is to say the other'.[273] The essential problem remains understanding what the pre-condition of multiculturalism is, or, to use a phrase that has fallen out of use, what its founding values are.

There are those, like Sandel, who remind us that the primacy of what is right over good is founded 'on the primacy of the self over ends, values, social attachments'. But this primacy, to really understand it, 'is unacceptable because we cannot construct our identity independently of the ends and the values of the community to which we belong'.[274] And everything should be placed in a framework of stability without which such values could not be fully experienced and the 'others', to whom we constantly relate, would end up by losing their forms of security and therefore their differences and identities by which everyone ends up, or can end up, enriching themselves.

'Identity should not be thought of as fixed'. Culture in its etymological meaning, as well, should be thought of as something in movement. Identities should be 'thought of as pluralities in constant contact with a mix of us with the other'. Hence a new idea of citizenship that 'always tends to cross over the territorial limits of a citizenship immune to the diaspora of a shared future'. However we may want to comment on these statements, it is certain that today we are faced with 'fluid identities that are connected, with the danger of a forced relocation which stiffens them to the point of making them precipitate into fundamentalisms'.[275]

---

273 *Ibid.*, p. 40.
274 Cf. *ibid.*, pp. 41ff.
275 Cf. *ibid.*, pp. 49-50 and 48.

2. Ethnicity: values and dangers

'Modernity is universalism, rationalisation; but it is also the affirmation of individual identity, the upholding of collective identities, first of all national and religious collective identities' Who could not agree with such a conclusion that also has the feature of involving a difficult achievement? However, we should reflect attentively on the meaning of ethnicity. This is marked by 'the affirmation of ourselves as substantially belonging to an inherited lineage, to a shared history or memory'.[276] These are aspects that for a 'foreigner' are increasingly acquiring a growing value.

The affirmation of ethnicity 'can follow different pathways': a) it can ask for 'the defence to the utmost of its own cultural boundaries', folding in on a general theory of multiculturalism; b) it can make 'the request for recognition of difference combining this with principles of a universalistic nature' (various human rights, rights to equal opportunity, etc.); and c) it can, lastly, induce 'a frontal clash' and in the most extreme cases be a reason for civil war or anyway a war between groups of organised crime.[277] Why can all of this happen? The fact is that multi-ethnicity is not a mere synonym for multiculturalism as it now seems to be understood in daily life.

To this is added 'that identity differences are not of the same nature as economic-social differences, and their recognition raises rather complex questions',[278] not least

---

276 Cf. S. Tabboni, 'Lo straniero e il dibattito contemporaneo sulla democrazia', in F. Crespi and R. Segatori, *Multiculturalismo e democrazia* (Donzelli Editore, Rome, 1996), p. 126. The author rightly refers to the work of A. Touraine, *Critique de la modernité*.

277 Cf. *ibid.*, p. 127. See also M. Wieviorka, *La Démocratie à l'épreuve. Nationalisme, populisme, ethnicité* (La Découverte, Paris, 1993).

278 Cf. *ibid.*, p. 129.

because, more than removing obstacles, most of the time one is dealing with reaching objectives. To sum up, reconciling multi-ethnicity and multiculturalism appears increasingly difficult.[279] To avoid certain dangers, which are always latent, we should really speak about a new universalism that is able to temper the excesses of multiculturalism in order to avoid the disintegration of social reality.[280]

Probably we need to recognise that at the roots of these problems there is a basic misunderstanding. To clarify this one can start from an observation made by Donati: 'Citizenship was primarily – in ancient and traditional societies – *political and juridical* (political rights), and then with the modern epoch above all *economic* (civil rights and then welfare rights)'. All of this is no longer sufficient because, today, it has 'become *social* in a sense that is not in the least different: according to the semantics of *human rights*'. For this reason, leaving aside every 'temporal' reference – which from a cultural perspective could subtend the ideas of progress or evolution – we should speak about a 'societal' citizenship: a *societal complex of relationships*, also called post-modern citizenship, with some continuities with modern citizenship. [281]

This new definition, which I find more philosophical than sociological, leads me to emphasise that the word 'society', at the basis of the new adjective of citizenship, implies a *prius* on which we should agree to obtain basic rules that

---

279 Cf. A. Ferrara (ed.), *Comunitarismo e liberalismo* (Editori Riuniti, Rome, 1992), p. LV.

280 Cf. A. Ferrara, 'Multiculturalismo ben temperato e democrazia', in F. Crespi and R. Segatori, *Multiculturalismo e democrazia*.

281 Cf. P. Donati, 'La cittadinanza democratica fra particolarismo e nuovo universalismo', in F. Crespi and R. Segatori, *Multiculturalismo e democrazia*, pp. 192-193. See also P. Donati, *La cittadinanza societaria* (Franco Angeli, Milan, 1993).

are at the basis of any civil consortium. For a society to exist some shared intentions should be at its basis, without which society itself disintegrates. [282] Contrary elements must also be referred to basic reasons and to paraphrase Kant to a certain extent unsociability must be made sociable in order to implement the classic principle of *concordia discors*, which Lucan was already illustrating,[283] at the basis of the Roman idea of civic life.

When in civil society fractures exist which can increasingly expand between an ethnic group and the rest of society, one could run the risk of generating phenomena of a mafia kind or, anyway, organised crime. The mafia, and this is no accident, is increasingly becoming an international phenomenon that no longer refers to a specific reality but to a sociological phenomenon. One thus creates an 'unwritten code of laws' which, however, regulates relationships within a particular reality of an ethnic kind. The top of the group, which is certainly not elected but has become established on the basis of self-referential systems, sub-divides the ethnic community and the territory in which it finds itself so as to control individual remunerative activities. Between this working group and the executive top of the uncontrolled 'ethnic group', where this has mafia characteristics, 'revolves a court of overseers' that live maintained by work activities to which various kinds of protection are assured.[284] The first effect is to remove resources from the state community in which the criminal group works, but the consequence is be withdrawn from control by authorities recognised by the majority.

---

282 Cf. R. Pezzimenti, *The Open Society and its Friends, with Letters from Isaiah Berlin and Karl R. Popper*, esp. ch. I.

283 Cf. *ibid.*, point 2.24.

284 Cf. A. Mastopaolo, 'Mafia', in N. Bobbio, N. Matteucci, G. Pasquino (eds.), *Dizionario di politica*, p. 555.

In this situation not only do people not take part in, and share the ideals of, multiculturalism but they are also strongly jealous about not polluting their own identity because it could end up 'out of control'. In this way is created along mafia lines an organisation of the whole of a complex universe of power that is alternative to the official version, which also re-proposes its bureaucracy that, obviously, has to be maintained. The control of commercial activity, in which those who do not accept the rules do not survive, then generates almost a parallel 'civil' society that regulates justice in its own way.[285] The control of the territory reaches its peak when the real estate market of the area is controlled, that is to say the area in which the ethnic community that has not wanted to integrate works, ignoring the appeals, albeit of a flattering kind, of multicultural universalism.

There is thus achieved an authentic enclave within a community that nonetheless has the canons of acceptance and multiculturality. Speculation, the desire to get rich, an iron hierarchy able to prevail against the weakest, and as a consequence exploitation and fear that become evident only with difficulty,[286] are the final requirements of this rejection of the multicultural vision which instead is escaped from. The tops of these groups usually exercise a very private system of co-option, unless internal violence does not aim at redesigning the organogram of the ethnic group. When signs of openness appear to bubble up in these groups, most of the time they are dictated by the need to enlarge their sphere of action and then links are sought that can allow this.

This is a danger to which today all those democracies that exchange an approach of guarantees with permissiveness are exposed. Today there are too many who believe that

---

285 Cf. *ibidem*.

286 Cf. *ibid.*, p. 556.

democracies defend themselves against themselves, that they are endowed with infallible cultural anti-bodies and do not adequately support their institutions. And when the phenomenon of organised crime acquires uncontrollable characteristics it becomes if not impossible at least extremely expensive, in terms of human lives as well, to react and to place a territory under control once again. This is not to mention that the ethnic groups that completely avoid insertion usually have a provenance and often a support derived from States that are certainly not weak and have expansionist aims.

XII. TRUTH AND DEMOCRACY: CAN ONE DO WITHOUT FOUNDATIONS?

'The conclusion that I seek to arrive at is that the farewell to truth is the beginning, and the very basis, of democracy. If there was an *objective* truth of social and economic laws (economics is not a natural science), democracy would be a completely irrational choice'. This conclusion is the outcome of a premise that runs through all the thought of Vattimo: 'the question of truth is acknowledged to be a question of interpretation'.[287] To sustain this thesis, Vattimo himself says that it would be enough to think of the dramatic experience of the war in Iraq, to justify which politicians like Bush and Blair engaged in 'lies about the weapons of mass destruction of Saddam'[288] in order to make people believe in the purity of their intentions.

'This example demonstrates how today politicians and politics allow themselves many violations of ethics and thus also of the duty to speak the truth without anyone being scandalised'.[289] Such a statement, however, forgets certain assumptions of crucial importance. The *first* is that such an approach refers back to a precise itinerary of thought that, and not only today, has tended to replace the logic of the true with the logic – which then turns out to be ephemeral – of success. The *second*, which is banal and perhaps for this

---

287 G. Vattimo, *Addio alla verità*, (Meltemi Editore, Rome, 2009), pp. 16 and 15.

288 *Ibid.*, p. 7.

289 *Ibid.*, p. 8.

reason ignored by overly acute minds, is connected to the fact that the lies 'willed' by politicians do not invalidate the truth but, rather, keep it hidden.

Then there is a *third* assumption, to explain which one should bear in mind another observation of Vattimo: if we wanted to have a vision of truth in politics 'it would be better to entrust the State to experts, to the philosopher kings of Plato or the Nobel prize-winners of all the various disciplines'. However, this conclusion starts from the belief that when speaking about truth it is, once again from a purely Hegelian perspective, 'a vision that escapes partiality' and for this reason imposes 'a social transformation that can end up only in totalitarianism'.[290] That the organ of the Leninist Party, specifically in a Hegelian key, was *Pravda*, that is to say 'Truth', should make us reflect. But this truth, which for very many was *synonymous* with democracy, albeit of a proletarian kind, has nothing to do with what we now mean by truth. Indeed it generated a system, as I believe I have demonstrated elsewhere,[291] that was synonymous with *deformation and lying*. It is also worthwhile remembering that totalitarianisms exchanged truth, and alas also morality, for what could turn out to be a sort of 'tyranny of the majority', thereby transforming the approach of individual success into the no less dangerous approach of collective success. This is how we should understand the 'party as a modern prince' of Gramsci, which, understood in these terms, seems to be anything but 'a step ahead in the direction of democracy'.[292] This is a thesis advanced by a significant number of scholars.[293]

---

290 *Ibid.*, p. 10.

291 Cf. R. Pezzimenti, *Politica e religione. La secolarizzazione nella modernità*.

292 G. Vattimo, *Addio alla verità*, p. 14.

293 Cf. amongst many other works L. Pellicani, *Gramsci e la questione comunista* (Vallecchi Editore, Florence, 1976).

1. Between scepticism and realism

One of the most relevant reasons why contemporary philosophy opposes the very idea of truth is that it finds it permeated with a metaphysical charge that today is seen, at the least, as unfashionable. This belief is due above all else to the hermeneutic outlook. The consequence is very clear: 'Truth is thus made to coincide not with the truth of being but with the interpretation of truth, in a radical overturning of the metaphysical notion of truth as *adaequatio*'.[294] Certainly, notwithstanding Heidegger, this does not mean the end of metaphysics but 'only' its superseding. This term, in the contemporary 'cultural' vision, is almost synonymous with annihilation.

The truth no longer has a founding meaning but, given that we have moved from the idea that being constitutes truth to the idea that at the most sees being as an interpretation, we are faced with 'multiple interpretations of truth due to the character of the being that is uncovered (*the ontology of the inexhaustible* of Pareyson)'. Even before discussing the plausibility of such a position, we should ask ourselves, St. Augustine would say, whether this search for truth is 'a search that continues in truth and is not outside truth'.[295] In other terms, I am prepared to speak about truth as an achievement or broadening, but can this search be engaged in blindly with all the risks that history has amply demonstrated? Can we navigate, as some say without a direction, but also without a port that we come from and above all are headed for?

The posing of these questions for some contemporary thinkers is incorrect because it involves returning to speak

---

[294] G. Mura, 'La 'verità' nella prospettiva ermeneutica', in V. Possenti (ed.), *La questione della verità. Filosofia, scienze, teologia* (Armando Editore, Rome, 2003), p. 209.

[295] *Ibid.*, pp. 210 and 212.

about truth as *adaequatio*. However, in this case 'there is no diminution of the hermeneutic notion of truth as openness to infinite meanings of being, of the spirit and of the person which, rather, is enriched'. For that matter, it is this which allowed the human sciences not only to be founded but also to develop.[296] And we should not forget the important contributions made by epistemology 'as a discipline that deals with the foundations of the sciences and the typical way by which they know'. It is certainly the case that all of this has brought about 'a pluralistic fragmentation' of the concept of truth which is seen as a multiplicity of perspectives in which 'one can know and describe reality'.[297] However, it would be erroneous to reduce the question of truth to the level of science, philosophy and theology, forgetting that the question of truth affects our daily lives. Indeed, conventional wisdom has to deal with truth and arguments, in the same way as the questions and issues that derive from them are not – as I will attempt to demonstrate – less important.

To address the question I will start, in order to summarise, from how dictionaries define truth. Truth in them is seen in terms of some of its possible aspects: '1) truth as correspondence or conformity between thought and reality; 2) truth as manifestation, openness, what is evident, direct contact; 3) truth as divine revelation; 4) truth as consistency; 5) truth as conformity to a rule; 6) truth as inter-subjective consensus; 7) truth as utility and efficacy'.[298] I will not

---

[296] *Ibid.*, pp. 216 and 214.

[297] Cf. V. Possenti, 'La domanda sulla verità e i suoi concetti', in V. POSSENTI (ed.), *La questione della verità. Filosofia, scienze, teologia*, pp. 15-16.

[298] Cf. V. Possenti, 'Verità', in *Dizionario Interdisciplinare Scienza e Fede*, edited by G. Tanzella Nitti and A. Strumia (Urbaniana University Press-Città Nuova Editrice, Rome, 2002) pp. 1502-1518.

consider the last four points of this sub-division, namely 4 to 7, which, in my view, demonstrate how necessary truth is to the normality of daily life, specifically because of that *primum vivere* that then allows us to analyse greater questions. As regards point 1), I fully agree with what Dummett argues: 'the realist has a lot more to say for himself'[299] than – I would add – his detractors.

I would like to immediately point out that I accept a simple but crucial definition of realists: 'that is to say, people who think that there is a way in which things are, independently of the fact of whether one knows or can know that they are like that'.[300] Following this, it would be more 'useful to distinguish between truth, belief, knowledge and certainty',[301] but for now let us remain with the seven above-mentioned points.

Point 6), *truth as inter-subjective agreement*, reminds us that any inquiry into truth involves those who live and share with us a certain type of experience, to the point that the search for truth involves our way of understanding our relationships with others – relationships that are very often shaped by our way of understanding and living truth. 'Wittgenstein argued that without such public norms, norms shared by a group and constituting a form of life,

---

[299] M. Dummet, *Truth and Other Enigmas* (Duckworth, London, 1978), p. 24.

[300] D. Marconi, *Per la verità. Relativismo e filosofia* (Giulio Einaudi Editore, Turin, 2007), p. 3.

[301] Bearing in mind that it would be useful to make a distinction, the quotation continues: 'that our use of the word 'true' is governed by certain requirements and those who do not respect them are speaking about something else; that scepticism is probably irrefutable, but on the other hand it is sustainable only at very high theoretical costs; that it is difficult to speak about 'relativism' without further clarifications; that many forms of relativism are incompatible with the idea that tolerance is an absolute value; and so forth': *ibid.*, pp. VI-VII.

language and even thought itself would be impossible'.[302] It is certainly the case that such rules should be seen from a dynamic point of view, but it is equally undoubted that such dynamism springs from the premises that make it possible.

In this case that truth also becomes an 'existential disposition' and a way of understanding the other, an 'interpersonal dialogic openness' that is able to see existence as being able to fulfil itself in truth, in the 'knowledge of the inexhaustibility of the true'. In this approach we have presented to us 'truth as discovery'.[303] This 'inexhaustible journey' towards truth is stimulated by a need generated by truth itself to the point that the question of truth as a *prius aut posterius* emerges as something that cannot be avoided or eliminated, as well as being inexhaustible.

If we understand things aright, it could not be otherwise given that the 'logical process of *establishing* the truth of every discourse inevitably leads to the *evidence* of an original nucleus of experiential certainties that have an ultimately founding character'.[304] Indeed, nobody can withdraw from this position, not even a sceptic who can doubt, and in fact doubts, everything, except his self. Putnam rightly argues: 'That [total] relativism is inconsistent is a truism amongst philosophers. After all, is it not *obviously* contradictory to *hold* a point of view while at the same time holding that *no* point of view is more justified or right than any other?'[305]

---

302 H. Putnam, *Reason, Truth and History* (Cambridge University Press, 1981), p. 107.

303 Cf. V. Possenti, 'La domanda sulla verità e i suoi concetti', p. 19.

304 A. Livi, 'Dalla logica formale alla logica aletica. La nozione filosofica di 'senso comune' per una fondazione rigorosa della verità del discorso', in V. Possenti (ed.), *La questione della verità. Filosofia, scienze, teologia*, p. 240.

305 H. Putnam, *Reason, Truth and History*, p. 119. The text in squared brackets is mine.

To be clear, this is a little like those who argue that truth does not exist, or that nothing is true and everything is possible, without realizing that they are making a statement that claims, in its turn, to be true. Scepticism in this way, as well, starts from a *first founding statement*. This is why, really to be consistent, one should say with Putnam 'if it is true that only statements that can be criterially verified can be rationally acceptable, that statement itself cannot be criterially verified, and hence cannot be rationally acceptable'.[306]

Conventional sense, which has a greater propensity to understand daily life, *can add other statements* to this *first founding statement*. Life offers statements of truth that are acceptable to the light of simple common sense and it seems absurd that the methodology of philosophers cannot understand them. I remember a countryman who had a barrel that he wanted to clean. A young man was holding the upper lid of the barrel in his hand and did not know where to put it. The countryman looked at him and said. "If the lid belongs to the barrel, you will have to put it somewhere and it will certainly fit the barrel. Remember that a part is never greater than the whole. This is a *truth that nobody can doubt*". Afterwards he added: "Try to understand this before you die, for sooner or later we all have to die. This is *a further truth* that nobody can deny".

To return to the points listed above, one may say that truth understood as 'unveiling and truth as conformity are not in the least incommensurable or opposed to each other, the first is the pre-condition for the second and at the same

---

[306] *Ibid*, p. 111. It should not be forgotten that this American philosopher moves within a position typical of realism: 'Putnam conserves the realist insight that truth is independent of justification or acceptance *here and now*, even it is not independent of *any* justification': S. Veca, 'Premessa' to H. Putnam, *Reason, Truth and History*; Italian edition: *Ragione, verità e storia*, p. VIII.

time must necessarily be achieved in it'.[307] The fact that from this point of view truth can never be learnt in a definitive way does not mean that truth does not exist but only that our way of drawing near to it is partial and depends on our way of knowing it or portraying it. In essential terms, the fallibilist approach itself of Popper does nothing else but confirm what we can hold to be an 'itinerary' towards truth, an itinerary that concerns ourselves and not truth in itself. Expressed in other terms, truth can be stable but this is not true of our way of understanding it. This is the 'meliorist' position of fallibilism and not the position, obviously enough, that understands it as the standard-bearer of scepticism.[308] For that matter, it was Popper himself who saw it as such when, in speaking about Tarski, he came to say that having rehabilitated the much maligned theory of truth as correspondence, he had rehabilitated what Popper himself defined as the common sense idea of truth.[309]

2. Truth as a political question

Truth is frightening because, in the opinion of some, it is strongly in contrast with freedom. This is because between 'truth and domination there is not extraneousness, only perfect coinciding'.[310] This is because a 'foundationist' thesis is said to be equally 'fundamentalist'. Apart from the accuracy of such a conclusion, it *could be* true in the event that a philosophy created its own truth or this truth were the outcome of human acting alone, as it was for the

---

307 V. Possenti, 'La domanda sulla verità e i suoi concetti', pp. 21-22.

308 Cf. *Ibid.*, p. 37.

309 Cf. K.R. Popper, *Unended Quest. An intellectual Autobiography* (Fontana/Collins, Glasgow, 1982), p. 98.

310 U. Galimberti, 'La verità come efficacia', in *Sulla verità*, edited by M. Donà, *Paradosso*, nn. 2-3/1997 (Il Poligrafo, Padua, 1998), p. 63.

various Hegelian schools.[311] Yet other truths exist such as those of the future of nature which we can only confine ourselves to observing in order to try to discover their true sense and meaning, but which we ourselves certainly do not found.[312] We could say that the truths of nature also belong *to point 4)*, in the sense that nature relates in a consistent way with its laws whether we know them or do not know them.

Perhaps to be honest we should say that nature's consistency with its own laws (we are here still *at point 4)* must be total to ensure that everything functions. Our criterion of consistency is different. Above all if we remain *in the domain of truth as discovery*, in us 'consistency is understood not as nature of the truth but as its criterion'. This is because there is a 'difference between *totally true* and the *whole of truth*: an assertion can be totally true and constitute a minuscule fraction of the whole truth'.[313]

Point 6), truth as inter-subjective agreement, imposes other considerations. Although it remains true that 'it is of a public character in the sense that true assertions can and must be justified publicly', the fact remains here,

---

311 I refer the reader once again to my *Politica e religione. La secolarizzazione nella modernità*, observing the claims to be in 'Truth' advanced by various dialecticians of the Right or the Left and, where this is necessary and according to choice, the Centre.

312 It is curious that on this point Marx, for a moment abandoning Hegelian dialectical prejudices, anticipates precisely what I argue here. Speaking evidently with Italian exiles, this German philosopher came to argue that, as Vico says, the history of humanity is marked out from the history of nature by the fact that we made the former and not the latter: K. Marx, *Capital. A Critical Analysis of Capitalistic Production*, volume I, translated by S. Moore and E. Aveling, (Lawrence & Wishart, London, 1974), p. 352, note 2. Subsequently this long note was taken up by the needs of dialectics in which nature as well as humanity was seen as being involved.

313 V. Possenti, 'La domanda sulla verità e i suoi concetti', pp. 37 and 36.

as well, that their value is not exhausted at the moment of 'publicity'. Indeed, they constitute the premise of a possible civil life that must be based on the truth of human relationships, to the point of being able to say that each person has the right to truth.

The right to truth, on a par with other rights, founds civil life. Otherwise, why should we require the truth about their contents or their origins to be written 'honestly' on food products? Why should we require the witnesses of a trial to say the truth that they know, without which the sentences could be invalid? Or again: why should we require politicians to tell the truth? In essential terms, even those who argue that truth is impossible, when the occasion arises require it. One need only think here that when we consult an 'expert', for example on health, we require that they should be sincere and rigorous, that is to say that they should tell the truth that they know.

It is certainly the case that when speaking about truth as inter-subjective agreement one can run a serious risk; indeed, one does run a serious risk. One can witness a 'deflation' of the question of truth that could be circumscribed to the contingent, thereby removing its characteristics of universality or inability to be denied that it should have. In this case, truth becomes instrumental in the sense that for its exponents it is able not only to affect but also to 'change' society. The paladin of this position is Dewey who even speaks about thought as directed acting. This occurs because, albeit unconsciously, one then ends up in the footsteps of Rorty by accepting 'the assumption that ideas and language are only tools to meet one's own needs'.[314] One thus falls into a neo-pragmatism that reduces truth to utility that turns point 6) into point 7) – truth as utility and efficacy.

---

314 *Ibid.*, pp. 40-41.

In this case, however, one should be careful not to get stuck in a turbid equivocation. Indeed, we are rightly reminded by Livi that we cannot forget 'the distinction between *certainty* (which is the relationship of the subject to the evident reality of the truth of their own thought) and *consensus* (which is the possible result of communication through language)'.[315] *Consensus*, to which obviously the Western tradition has attributed an uncontested value (one may refer here to the farsighted vision of Cicero),[316] remains, however, a fundamental rule of the democratic game. One is indeed dealing with a game because although it is decisive for democratic life, it can certainly not see itself as immune to errors and, at times, contrary to truth. In other words, agreement can err in a dramatic fashion.

What has just been said finds 'ironic' confirmation in the book *On Bullshit* of Harry Frankfurt, a work published a few years ago. The person whom we could define as its 'protagonist', the bullshitter, is not a liar when it comes to the truth (otherwise it would be easy to unmask him), but, rather, a man who argues in favour of a belief – ignoring whether it is true or false – with the sole aim of convincing other people. He is a sort of opinion leader who is not concerned about the accuracy of his opinions. He only knows that in a society reduced to a talk show, what matters is to find agreement. It is precisely this that Vattimo advances: for him the agreement of the community can be separate from what is true or false. The important thing is to create a community in agreement.

---

315 A. Livi, 'Dalla logica formale alla logica aletica. La nozione filosofica di 'senso comune' per una fondazione rigorosa della verità del discorso', p. 232.

316 Cf. R. Pezzimenti, *The Open Society and its Friends, with Letters from Isaiah Berlin and Karl R. Popper*, 1,28.

It has been rightly observed[317] that Vattimo, in the footsteps of Bloch, believes that the only difference between a madman and a prophet lies in the capacity that the latter has to create a community. In truth, it seems to me, madmen have also created communities, whose tragic effects are before everyone's eyes.

As regards the authoritarian implications of truth, it is perhaps gainful to remember 'that totalitarian regimes are always inclined systematically to deny even the most obvious truths'. In addition, in the case of where scientific truths are taken as paradigms, Vattimo argues that *'what is held up as truth is nothing else but interpretation'*. However, it was rightly pointed out to him that such an approach is shown to be groundless when it seeks to consider the relationship between science and religion in terms of conflict. It is asserted, in fact, that the Catholic Church, with its 'claims based upon Christian mythology', counters the atheistic impact of science and ends up by denying the claims to objectivity – and thus to truth – of science. This contradicts the premise of the discourse because since science should not have 'legitimate claims to truth but is only one interpretation like any other, why should the Church not oppose them, in the same way, with its alternative descriptions of reality?' As another corollary, one could further deduce: 'if the vision of the Christian world is not in competition with science, what reason is there for denying the truth of science?'[318]

It is logical that after abandoning the very idea of truth we return to what has just been advanced: *'what is held up as truth is nothing else but interpretation'*.

---

317 Cf. D. Marconi, 'Senza verità siamo più liberi?', in *Il Sole 24 Ore*, 7 June 2009, n. 155, p. 35. This review is excellent and penetrating, at times more than palatable.

318 *Ibidem*.

Everything, including philosophy, is reduced to a tale reinterpreted with the 'eyes' of those who tell it. This translates what by now seems to have become an adagio: 'facts do not exist – only interpretations'. Here, as well, however, we cannot avoid posing a question: *from where do interpretations come*, from other interpretations or, in the final analysis, from facts? In other words, 'interpreting' *what and on what bases*? What is the subject of interpretation? And then there is a question that worries me even more: can an interpretation not radically change a fact itself?

An example can clarify matters. About ten years ago, a TV news broadcast, reporting on a demonstration at Porta Pia in Rome to commemorate 20 September 1870, actually said that the commander of the Italian forces, who had just entered the city, sent a telegram to Cavour to communicate the success of the mission. I indignantly telephoned RAI (the Italian state TV network) to say that Cavour had died nine years previously! They answered that these broadcasts were made by news and general journalists who were not obliged to know the history of Italy! The next day I told my students about the broadcast but not the reason for my indignation and to my great surprise none of them was amazed at the absurdity of that news! For almost all the viewers, Cavour was still alive on 20 September 1870! Can interpretations, including erroneous ones, radically alter the truth of a fact?

Heidegger himself would also say that the truth of death, of that specific death and on that specific date, escapes any possible interpretation as a fact in itself. I would say that a fact exists, separately from any possible interpretation. Ignorance is as dangerous to truth as lying. And yet if the facts were left to mere hermeneutics,[319] to an interpretation detached from what is true, we could run gross risks. 'The history of men could appear to be a tale told by an idiot'.[320] To paraphrase Dummett, we could say that I no longer know 'whether it could be held that...You cannot change the past'.[321] Unfortunately, inventions have been perpetrated on history. Therefore, we should not complain if history, which could be a teacher for our lives, does not have disciples.

One easily understands that here we have a *quid pro quo*. For this reason, it has been rightly said that one remains 'with the impression that the post-modern analyst allows himself to appeal to the facts as much as the non-post-modern analyst, except to remind those who in order to counter post-modernist arguments appeal in their turn to the facts (perhaps of a rather brazen kind), that there are no facts but only interpretations'.[322] This is a position, as one can see, that is rather ridiculous.

Those who say that facts do not exist in reality produce an insuperable dichotomy. 'In effect it is impossible to know anything about the real if at the outset one places an unbridgeable ditch between the knower and the known'.[323] The knower finds himself, without knowing

---

319 I here take the opportunity to emphasise, as my dear friend Paolo Armellini wrote to me and which I obviously agree with, that 'the hermeneutics is not only that of Vattimo. In him the post-Marxist nihilism of Nietzsche which contently inhabits opulent society is radicalised. But the language has a relationship of a non-instrumental kind with truth'.

320 D. Antiseri and G. Vattimo, *Ragione filosofica e fede religiosa nell'era postmoderna* (Rubbettino Editore, Soneria Mannelli, 2008), p. 39.

321 M. Dummett, *Truth and Other Enigmas*, p. 350.

322 D. Marconi, *Per la verità. Relativismo e filosofia*, p. 80.

323 V. Possenti, 'Verità', in *Dizionario Interdisciplinare Scienza e Fede*, p. 1517.

why, in a darkened world that he encounters difficulty in understanding. One should ask oneself, at this point, *why should I respect it* given that it could be inexistent or the outcome of an erroneous interpretation? It is obvious that this is an anti-realist vision that has the presumption to affirm that in our contact with reality we discover only what we have already placed in things.

The fallibism of Popper itself, if understood correctly, combats this fashionable anti-realism. Indeed, let us remember that theories are our inventions, the outcome of our thought, but it is reality that makes them fail precisely when they are unable to relate to reality. Fallibism, like the verification method of Galileo, cannot do without reality, facts and events. Indeed, to criticise post-modern practitioners of hermeneutics, we could say that *one fact can be sufficient to put a hundred interpretations into a state of crisis.*

All of this is not enough. It would be interesting to know from those like Vattimo who argue that religion is not the bearer of truths but, rather, the promoter of charity, what they mean by this at times misunderstood word. If charity, as they hold, means respect and love for other people, then these last (other people), albeit in a reductive way, should become the foundation or, if one wants, the yardstick, of charity itself.

It appears, however, that Vattimo himself is aware of all of this when he observes: 'Christianity, indeed, has taught us that truth without charity has no sense'.[324] So truth has a foundation! If such is the case, we have to understand this as well. Let us try to do so with the same words as Vattimo for whom the Church can be the founding criterion of charity itself. One need only read carefully what follows:

---

324 G. Vattimo, 'Una bioetica post-metafisica', in D. Antiseri and G. Vattimo, *Ragione filosofica e fede religiosa nell'era postmoderna*, p. 11.

'less banal is the discourse on the authority of the Church since I cannot but recognise that the sacred texts to which I refer and want to interpret have been handed down to me only by a living tradition, and that on this basis I can also uphold the right to teach how they should be interpreted'.[325] However, Vattimo goes beyond this and as regards charity believes that today its real meaning is a matter of free interpretation since 'in the Gospel all the law and the prophets are reduced to two commandments: *love God above all things and your neighbour as yourself*'.[326] What surprises me is that we repeat this phrase, *which is to say the least fundamental*, not dwelling on the fact that it sums up all the law and the prophets, which Christ perfected. The saints, and the whole of the mystical tradition, understood this well and sought to put into practice the real counsel of Jesus: 'love one another as I have loved you'. The difference is not a small one. It is by this second commandment – *and this is taught by the whole of the discourse of the Last Supper* – that conversion is measured. The *first* sums up the Old Testament and for Christ it is incomplete. It does not yet present the Cross which appears in the *second*, and whether we like this or not, it is the Cross that saves us. Only if we accept this measurement of love, this 'foundation', do we accept our conversion to Christ, otherwise we would want Christ's conversion to us.

3. Truth and law: why speak about inalienable rights and conscientious objection?

From what has been said hitherto there springs a distinction that is certainly not futile or of secondary importance. Davidson argues that 'there are important

---

325 G. Vattimo, *Credere di credere* (Garzanti, Milan, 1996), p. 88.

326 *Ibid.*, p. 79.

differences between theories of relative, and of absolute, truth, and the differences make theories of the two sorts appropriate as answers to different questions'.[327] As regards the *first theories*, the parameters of reference become fundamental and to the point that it can be said: 'It is difficult to see how a theory of meaning can hope to succeed that does not elucidate, and give a central role to, the concept of reference'. The *second theories* are much more complex because in this case 'there are weighty reasons for supposing that reference cannot be explained or analysed in terms more primitive or behavioural',[328] and, I would say, in complete and exhaustive terms.

Before seeing how much the theories of relative truth are fundamental in democratic life, we should not neglect another simple observation made by Davidson. Why should we be interested in what happens around us? Perhaps because we are convinced that scepticism is a disguised form of selfishness that is unable to address the problems that spring from 'being together'? Whatever the case may be: 'Philosophical interest in facts springs partly from their promise for explaining truth...To specify a fact is, then, a way of explaining what makes a sentence true'.[329] Certain assumptions about being together, about our civil life and also about our democracy, underlie these observations.

Laws themselves refer back to a corpus of values inscribed in the fundamental charter of a people. But a Constitution, in its turn, refers to certain assumptions drawn from the tradition of that people itself. Amongst these assumptions, the moral and the religious, with their

---

327 D. Davidson, *Inquiries into Truth and Interpretation* (Oxford University Press, New York, 1985), p. 69.

328 *Ibid.*, p. 215.

329 D. Davidson, *Essays on Actions and Events* (Oxford University Press, New York, 1985), p. 130.

'metaphysical' approaches as well, as we know from the epoch of Montesquieu not to say that of Cicero, play a primary role. Constitutions themselves cannot go against these principles, precisely because they constitute the founding criteria of those inalienable rights that every Constitution must respect. It is certainly the case that from this point of view it is absurd to believe that only that action is valid that conforms to positive law, as is asserted by the pure doctrine of positive law. I am also fully aware that this position clashes with certain convictions derived from the school of Kelsen and from other juridical and political approaches However, there are also various examples that demonstrate the contrary.

If Constitutions could ignore those rights that they define as founding when they are generated, how could one speak of inalienable rights? The fact is that for some decades, unfortunately, we have 'all' become to a certain extent disciples of Kelsen. We have been trying to 'purify' jurisprudence[330] ever since it was 'hybridised' with other disciplines such as psychology, ethics, theology and yet others. Is all of this possible? Such a doubt seems to traverse even the mind of Kelsen himself when he says that 'the norms of universal morality without doubt apply to all men...whereas juridical norms oblige and authorise only specific categories of men'.[331] It is licit to ask, therefore, why the first should not be seen to be higher than the second. The troubled history of dissent should demonstrate this to us amply. Is this not perhaps the confirmation that law has its bases in something that goes beyond the mere facts that it wants to regulate? How could

---

330 Cf. H. Kelsen, *Reine Rechtslehre. Einleitung in die rechtswissenschaftliche Problematik* (F. Deuticke Verlag, Vienna, 1934); Italian edition: *Lineamenti di dottrina pura del diritto*, edited by R. Treves (Giulio Einaudi Editore, Turin, 1996 seventeenth edition), p. 47.

331 *Ibid.*, p. 53.

we explain forms of conscientious objection if the conscience did not hold to be true certain motivations that are separate from the ability of law to be implemented? At this point we return to the arduous question of the right to truth. I am of the opinion that a juridical sense, rightly understood, cannot exist that is able to defend promises, and also premisses, that are false. Otherwise nobody could ensure the civil survival of any human aggregation. The very word 'society' indicates that it is constituted through the achievement and the implementation of these premisses.[332] This is confirmed by the fact that the 'forgetting of a promise does not invalidate the obligation to keep it. It should not have been forgotten'. To this one should add that a 'right is not extinguished if its possessor does not remember it'.[333] This means that certain principles must be separate from not remembering: whether a person remembers them or not, considers them or ignores them, they remain valid because they are true. Otherwise, how could an 'international court' condemn a government because it engaged in actions that did not go against its own legal system or its own ideological creed?

Let us remember that the right to truth is, in addition, the foundation of daily life. Every one of us invokes it with absolute rigour, for example when a product is eaten. The obligation to indicate the dates of production or expiry cannot be avoided, and the same may be said of the quality or the quantity of the components put into a product. Who could deny that this is one of the most elementary certainties of daily life? One is dealing with a right to truth, or, if one wants, not to be deceived, which nobody can and wants to

---

332 Cf. R. Pezzimenti, *The Open Society and its Friends, with letters from Isaiah Berlin and Karl R. Popper*, esp. the first chapter.

333 R. Spaemann, *Persone. Sulla differenza tra 'qualcosa' e 'qualcuno'*, p. 218.

forgo, not even those people who are not directly involved. One may think of the example of a trial: it is not only the contesting parties that invoke truth but also the person who is called to judge and resolve a dispute.

One may say, paradoxically, that the false, as well, leads to discovering truth because unmasking the false acts to identify the truth. Rightly 'it is correct to say that a judge must always decide on the basis of *trial truth*, but not that such truth is exclusively formal: trial truth is truth *tout court*, even if of necessity *perspective*, because of how the judge, from his point of observation, manages to understand it'.[334] On the other hand, why should we reopen trials that have already taken place with a 'sentence' if not because new 'sources' of truth have been acquired? Here we are not dealing at all with 'farewell to truth': without it we would be *condemned to the most total barbarity*.

Rosmini was right to say that 'it is right to say in general that each man, considering the vigour of his personality, the extension of connatural law, possesses the following rights: 1. To tell the truth'.[335] Others follow, but to conclude it is fitting to dwell upon this right. Telling the truth is not only a question of conscience that can be approached in a subjective way, some would say today in an 'interpretative' way. It is also, and above all else, a form of respect towards the other, the person who could be injured by us not telling the truth. 'From here it follows clearly that every attempt to deprive man of truth or virtue of happiness is an injury to formal law – the person'.[336] This is a confirmation that the person is truly subsistent law. To call into question such a truth is to call into question every other right of the person.

---

334 F. D'Agostino, *Giustizia. Elementi per una teoria* (Edizioni San Paolo, Cinisello Balsamo (MI), 2006), p. 56.

335 A. Rosmini, *Filosofia del diritto (1841-1843)*, vol. I, n. 147, p. 213.

336 *Ibid.*, n. 100, p. 201.

Truth is a concrete given fact that everyone wants to enjoy and must enjoy. Here the principle re-echoes that 'everyone wants the enjoyment of truth'. As a corollary, there comes from this the observation of having 'met many people who want to deceive, but nobody who wants to be deceived'.[337] We have before us a conclusion that cannot be neglected. The risk could be very grave. Those who deny it could be its first victims, experiencing what an anonymous writer of the Patristic age wrote: 'Liars will lie to themselves if they have no one to deceive'.[338]

---

337 Augustine (Sancti) *Confessionum libri tredecim*, in *Opera Omnia*, vol. I (Città Nuova Editrice, Rome, 1975), 10, 23, 33.

338 Anonimo, 'Opera incompleta su Matteo', in *La Bibbia commentata dai Padri. Nuovo Testamento 1/2. Matteo 14-28* (Città Nuova Editrice, Rome, 2006), p. 164.

XIII. POPULISM AND POPULARISM

The phenomenon of populism is certainly an ancient one even though in our epoch it has acquired various forms and is not always easy to define. Those who exalt this phenomenon seem, however, to have in common an 'idealised vision of the people' who are seen in the main almost 'in their original purity and harmony'. This almost always involves a 'feeling of anti-elitism which here I would define as a vague feeling of anti-representation'.[339] In this way, one tends to abolish the separation between representatives and the represented, given that the former are no longer able to perform their function.

1. Contemporary populism

In the 1980s there were those who argued that populism was also a sort of epithet by which to insult a political opponent who ended up by being held up to ridicule because he could not deal with an accusation that ended up by discrediting him. Hence the semantic opposition of *popular/populist* that advanced in all languages, as witness the Spanish and Portuguese *popular/populista*, the English *popular/populist*, the German *völkisch/*

---

339 I would like to refer the reader to chapter IV, 'Populismo e antiparlamentarismo', of my work R. Pezzimenti, *Il pensiero politico del XX secolo. La fine dell'eurocentrismo* (Rubbettino, Soneria Mannelli, 2013), pp. 111-170.

populistich, etc.³⁴⁰ If we see things correctly, there remains the fact, however, as is indicated by a winning phrase of Mény and Surel in the introduction to their successful study, that whatever the case 'populism' attests to a state of democratic malaise.³⁴¹

To be more precise, it is a form of risk for democracies and when it comes to their survival it is a lethal virus that cannot always be identified because it is able to disguise itself under appearances. Populism appears as a search for *hyper-democratic forms*, for idealised democracies available at a low cost and also easily achievable by ordinary citizens who are not very inclined to politics and can be transformed without much effort into active and piloted politicians.³⁴² This transformation is a necessity for populism which feels that it is combating, in the name and on behalf of ordinary people, the anonymity of the enemies of the people who use and take advantage of institutions. These institutions become increasingly demagogic and as a result more fragile. The tone of being tribunes that is characteristic of populists tends in addition to make 'professional' politicians appear increasingly distant from the daily needs of people, lost in the abstractness of useless and empty speeches. All of this takes place with the aim of increasingly discrediting the political class.³⁴³

---

340 Cf. W. Kraushaar, 'Die Neue Leutseligkeit', in H. Dubiel (ed.), *Populismus und Aufklärung* (Suhrkamp, Frankfurt am Main, 1986), pp. 278ff. I have doubts as to whether the 'popular/populist' tandem exists in the English language.

341 Cf. Y. Mény and Y. Surel, *Par le peuple, pour le peuple* (Fayard, Paris, 2000).

342 Cf. M. Tarchi, *L'Italia populista. Dal qualunquismo ai girotondi* (Il Mulino, Bologna, 2003), pp. 32-33.

343 Cf. *ibid.*, p. 28.

The contemporary phenomenon of populism certainly arose with the crisis of liberal democracies whose limitations were emphasised by it but soon forgotten by it. The attack on what was held to be the democracy of the bourgeoisie was launched by both the Right and the Left, even if today it is the attack launched by the Right that tends to be defined as populism. And yet a large dose of populism was a support for the Bolshevik revolution and to such an extent that Lenin stressed the fact that Russian populism was a form of protest against capitalism that was embodied in all those small local producers who had been ruined by capitalistic development.[344] In this way an *instinctive form* of political participation was born which bore witness – as Friedrich Jonas rightly points out[345] – to that crisis of reason that has characterised a part of contemporary history and also a class, namely intellectuals. Hence the impossibility of classifying – specifically because they are irrational – a series of elements that do not always make what happens completely decipherable.

In the light of what has been said, one can state that the first populism was characterised by its anti-bourgeois spirit, but given its irrationality it was transformed during the century and became an expression of the common people who became the heirs to the bourgeois spirit. These people felt that they were the bearers of a new feeling of 'community', of the spirit of a nation that led, above all in 'developing' countries, to nationalist ideals being united with ideals, of an apparently opposed character, of a socialist kind. The nationalisation of various – albeit backward – sectors of the economy demonstrates this fact. Perhaps, the most emblematic example of this was Peronism in Argentina.

---

344 Cf. R. Pezzimenti, *Il pensiero politico del XX secolo. La fine dell'eurocentrismo*, p. 113.

345 Cf. F. Jonas, *Geschichte der Soziologie* (Rowohlt Verlag GmbH, Reimbek bei Hamburg, 1968), chap. VI.

We should not neglect, and not only in developing countries, the just need for equality generated in contexts where inequalities had gone beyond the danger point. Hence an attack on a political class that did not manage to understand the frustrations of the honest part of the population. And perhaps in a more specific way the dissatisfaction and discontent towards a political system that has actors, and first of all political parties, that are insensitive to real problems or anyway unable to solve them.

It is specifically this inability that is concentrated on by those who want to achieve what have been defined as 'populist mobilisations', authentic reservoirs of what can become the populist electorate.[346] Those who accuse populism of aiming at political forms that do without parties and tend to eliminate the governing political class receive the reply that one is dealing here with direct democracy that wants to go beyond the old forms of representation and deprive the parties of space and power.

I want to say right away that I do not agree with this conclusion at all. Political parties have always been the first and fundamental expression of a democratic system. This is demonstrated by the aversion that over time they have had to overcome, in contexts deemed enlightened as well.[347] It is perhaps right to say that parties that are unable to channel needs, to voice innovations or to formulate adequate responses to impelling needs, accelerate that development of populism that constitutes the gravest accusation of their inefficiency. This can happen even when 'institutional or procedural instruments', which can channel the just needs for change, are lacking – to remain with the views of Mény

---

346 Cf. Y. Mény and Y. Surel, *Par le peuple, pour le peuple*, chap. VI.

347 Cf. amongst many studies L. Compagna, *L'idea dei partiti da Hobbes a Burke*.

and Surel. In short, when democracies are behindhand when it comes to the needs of society. As Dahl has rightly pointed out, a populist crisis takes place when a hiatus is created between ideal democracy and its practical implementation or, to put it even better, when certain fundamental rules of democratic government are called into question: '1. Control of the action of government is entrusted to the Constitution and elected representatives. 2. The representatives are chosen on the basis of electoral mechanisms at regular intervals and with fair procedures that exclude coercion. 3. The citizens have the right to express themselves freely without running the risk of being punished. 4. The citizens have the right to look for sources of independent and alternative information. 5. To ensure that everyone have their rights upheld, the citizens have the right to organise in groups and parties 6. No person who lives permanently in a country can see rights denied to them that are bestowed on the citizens'.[348] However this eclipse of rules is not always perceived in a clear way by people who, nonetheless, perceive that there is a political class that is different from the one it expects because it is unable to meet the expectations (which are not always clear) of those whose daily lives are difficult.

This 'opaqueness' has led some people to define populism as a 'syndrome', that is to say a state of mind characterised by symptoms, emotions and feelings. It is said not to have an ideology, a manifesto, a programme and not even precise programmes for the future. *The people are the depositary of truth* and for far too long a time have been

---

348 Cf. R. Pezzimenti, *Il pensiero politico del XX secolo. La fine dell'eurocentrismo*, p. 170. I refer here to R.A. Dahl, 'The Past and the Future of Democracy', *Occasional Papers, Cirap*, n. 5 (Sienna, 1999), p. 5.

the victims of swindles. It is a form of neo-pagan religion whose *divinity* is the people who worship themselves. *Satan* is that variegated and numerous set of adverse forces who try to swindle and compromise the people.[349]

With this point of view, Romano[350] rightly added that over the last two centuries populism has also been an expression of fears: it expresses a state of malaise caused by the trauma of change. It is unable to absorb the triple revolution (globalisation, ICT, bioethics) that has modified social equilibriums and endangers the standard of living of many people. It is sceptical about the future according to circumstances. In Europe, for example, it is Eurosceptic. Today it has also absorbed various groups of intellectuals and contesters or, whatever the case, of that Left that has had its trust in science and progress of a neo-Enlightenment kind weakened. One need only think of the way in which globalisation is addressed on the Left which, for example, forgets the idea of making proposals advanced by Marx himself. The Communist Manifesto pointed out how the bourgeoisie had for Marx by then taken on a role that went beyond States and individual governments. In its pages there is almost praise for what that class had managed to do in the world stage, going beyond narrow national boundaries and achieving an authentic 'internationalisation'.[351] Was it not for this reason that – in imitation and for the purposes of opposition – proletarians of the whole world were invited to unite?

---

349 Cf. L. Incisa, 'Populismo', in N. Bobbio, N. Matteucci and G. Pasquino, (eds.), *Dizionario di politica*, pp. 762ff.

350 Cf. S. Romano, 'Populisti per paura del nuovo', in *La Lettura/Corriere della Sera*, 7 April 2013.

351 On this subject cf. R. Pezzimenti, 'Globalizzazione: natura, vantaggi e contraddizioni', in F. Compagnoni and A. Lo Presto (eds.), *Etica e globalizzazione*, pp. 35-51.

2. A recurrent temptation

The temptation of direct democracy, which then increasingly becomes a 'summit democracy' as the experience of democratic centralism amply demonstrated, has always been waiting in ambush in history. It is really curious that its most enthusiastic proponents have been those who seek to cancel every metaphysical assumption of politics and then accept the more contestable assumption, that is to say the infallibility of a people that takes decisions without deep thought. It is symptomatic that specifically in the year 1922, at one of the most euphoric moments of populism, Capograssi wrote *La nuova democrazia diretta*. In this work the clear intention is to revise the concept itself of sovereignty which cannot be related to the cold logic of abstract legalism but must understand that 'by now a fatal transition from the State to the social body has taken place'.[352] Capograssi added that 'this is taking practical form and organising itself in great social interests'.[353]

These new social bodies, then as now, were the outcome of dynamics that had been underway for some time and were not in the least taken into account by institutions or abstract legal outlooks. Renewal required, and requires, 'the urgent need to envisage the transformation of the entire state system' in order to manage to 'understand' the new social realities and forces which otherwise would be marginalised and become extraneous to the political system, to the point of asking for new forms of direct participation. One thus understands the polyhedric importance of the verb 'to understand' which, in the first instance, means the need

---

352 N. Antonetti, 'Giuseppe Capograssi e la democrazia diretta', in G. Giunta (ed.), *La politica tra storia e diritto. Scritti in memoria di Luigi Gambino* (Franco Angeli, Milan, 2012), p. 29.

353 *Ibid.*, p. 29.

not to exclude anyone from a real process of change. One can respond to such pressing requests for democracy only by a legal recognition of new forms of participation that are able to incorporate what wants to exclude itself and engage in opposition. Only the acceptance of responsibility, which means first of all the possibility of having access to recognised and limited powers, can avoid populist negative developments.

To adapt, or better to innovate, once again in the domain of the limitation of powers constitutes the best weapon with which to save democracy. Furthermore, democracy survives as long as there really exist powers that are *super partes* and detached from populist arguments. I am thinking, for example, in Italy of the Head of State. Would his direct election by the people continue to make him, as he has been in the case of very many commendable figures, truly a point of reference for all the political and social forces? Would he not become a vulnerable premier like any other premier? Let us not forget that where direct forms of election exist, as in the USA, other organisms exist – I am thinking here of the Senate – that assure a certain political balance precisely because they are not the outcome of a simple calculation of the numerical majority in populist terms. Where certain organisms do not exist, one should be cautious in transforming certain institutions that could open up the way to easy forms of populism.

It is with this approach that one can summarise populism as being 'the natural resort of a society in crisis, fractured between the traditional sector and the modern sector'. This phenomenon, indeed, is typical of periods of transition, in which the need is perceived 'for appeals and coagulation with a high capacity of mobilisation'.[354] To summarise, it must be clear that populism tends to go beyond all forms

---

354 *Ibid.*, p. 767.

of representative democracy given that this last tends to place organisms of various kinds between the people and those who believe that they interpret the people in the most genuine way.

The concept of 'the people' is very different. The Romans linked the concept of a republic with its institutions, to which everyone had access, to this concept. Perhaps there has been rather little reflection, at least recently, on the formula *Senatus Populusque Romanus*. It indicates rather well[355] how the people, called to vote through the *comitia* and guided by their *tribunes*, could even gain access to the consulate. The people represented, so to speak, the democratic party, but it was tempered and limited by the aristocratic party of the *patres* present in the Senate. This organism, in its turn, was limited in a balance that imposed on every power a *sense of limits*. It is precisely this that is broken when populism triumphs. This also happened in the late Middle Ages when there was a shift from the crisis of the communes to lordship. The parties that opposed one another did not have the capacity to find alternative solutions and the winning formula seemed to be of a 'lord' called to deal with political events and supported by a majority and populist base.

It is superfluous to remember how it was precisely to this Roman approach that the English and American traditions referred,[356] limiting all attempts at demagoguery (along the lines of Rousseau that is to say). The aim was to avoid the triumph of the pure logic of numbers, which in an authentic democracy remains one of the decision-making instruments

---

355 I dedicated to this subject the first part of my work R. Pezzimenti, *The Open Society and its Friends, with Letters from Isaiah Berlin and the late Karl R. Popper*.

356 Cf.R. Pezzimenti, *The Open Society along the Arduous Path of Modernity, with Letters from Isaiah Berlin and Hilary Putnam*, chaps. 3 and 6.

and certainly not a claim to truth as is, in different fashion, the case with populism. This was put very well by De Gasperi[357] when he argued that a democracy has to be based on universal suffrage but remain representative.

3. How to get out of the swamp

These and other problems of representation have led to democracies to be spoken of as 'an unfinished process', with a 'systemic' crisis that involves various democratic countries to the point of calling into question 'the meaning of representative democracy'. It is certainly the case that 'crises never arrive suddenly' and the symptoms, particularly in Italy, touch upon the very foundations of representation: the oligopoly of parties and a blocked electoral system, low transparency in the management of public money, promises of constitutional reforms always not kept, and the passivity of citizens who are unable to exercise a real form of participation.

To move out of this stasis some people, like Robert Paul Wolff, have proposed so-called 'liquid democracy', a middle way between representative and direct democracy, in order to overcome the contradictions of parties. We have thus witnessed for a number of years various attempts at new forms of participation, the *Five Stars Movement* is the one that has most support, but we should not forget the *Indignados* in Spain or *Occupy Wall Street* in the USA. These movements, and in a special way the *Five Stars Movement*, are based above all else on two principles: 'the use of the Net and the system of delegation'.[358]

---

357 Cf. De Gasperi, *Idee sulla Democrazia Cristiana*, edited by N. Guiso (Edizioni Cinque Lune, Rome, 1974), p. 19.

358 Cf. F. Occhetta, 'La crisi della democrazia?', in *La Civiltà Cattolica*, anno 164, n. 3907, pp. 62-63.

A series of sound criticisms have been levelled against this model. First of all, 'those who control the means of discussion are able to direct and control votes and support'. It is added that 'the subjects of debate have multiplied excessively', bringing about difficulties as regards participation as well as disaffection and to such a point that 'the majority of electors run the risk of not knowing about the debates on the Net'. The real point that should be debated, it seems to me, however, is another: 'The form of the State that liquid democracy proposes is without intermediary bodies'.[359] I believe that these are the premisses, perhaps also the consequences, of very different problems from which those who care about democracy cannot retreat.

The first and most obvious is that *liquid democracy* tends towards very advanced forms of elitism because it tends to see the people as the people on the Net alone, even when this involves truly ridiculous numbers. Then it tends to make politics, naturally the 'politics of the Net', everything for citizens, as though they ended up by being limited to this new form of participation which, in essential terms, is reduced to an *exaggerated belief in ICT assemblies*. The references to certain wordings of the French Revolution should put us on our guard here. But above all it surprises me that not enough thought is directed to the ways and the times of the debates granted to an *ICT assembly*. Beyond the obvious – but not for this reason banal – danger of 'inconclusiveness', of which Hobbes was a brilliant prophet, the risk, and it is a serious one, is that emotion will prevail over rationality.

In addition, there is a further danger that should not be underestimated: the fact that an excessive transparency generates a more or less concealed sense of fear[360] or,

---

359 Cf. *ibid.*, p. 65.
360 On this subject see the insuperable work by G. Ferrero, *Potere. I*

anyway, of a forced homologation that is opposed to democracy. We should never tire of remembering that whereas authentic democratic systems conserve spaces of secrecy and confidentiality, for example the ballot, it has been authoritarian and totalitarian regimes that have sought excessive transparency that generates forms of repressive control. We should not forget that a crowd itself can as a subject become an object – 'crucify him! was the unanimous cry'[361] – and approve choices of an extremist character.

To summarise, democracy, even if we often ignore this fact, is a rather delicate mechanism, not least because, differently from other systems, it has to accept divisions, as long as these are not fatal to its on existence. Totalitarianism and authoritarianism have always been committed to avoiding and denying all divisions that could generate tensions and conflicts. However these last, if regulated and contained, are the essence of democracy, on the condition that everything is normalised by the ethics of conflict.

For this reason, non-democratic systems are opposed to the very idea of dialogue, not to speak of compromise, which they see as an insuperable obstacle to their establishment. Yet an authentic democracy, after a certain fashion, cannot do without healthy compromise. This is what is observed by Amy Gutmann and Dennis Thompson in their *The Spirit of Compromise*. If, as everybody knows, on 31 July 2012 there was an agreement between the two rival political parties in America to avoid a default, this means that at times one has to favour compromise rather than punishing it. There is another factor that should make us reflect. According to these two scholars, it is highly unlikely that a party will

---

Geni invisibili della Città, with an introductory essay by L. Pellicani (Sugarco Edizioni, Milan, 1981).

361 G. Zagrebelsky, *Il 'crucifige!' e la democrazia* (Giulio Einaudi Editore, Turin, 1995), p. 95.

obtain an absolute majority and if this were the case the divisions or contrasts would be within them. Discussion, a diversity of intentions and opinions, is the very nature of democracy. So why today is there so much hostility to compromise? Gutmann and Thompson identify three reasons. *First*: the ongoing electoral campaign. *Second*: the tendency of the mass media to follow politics as though it were a horse race. *Third*: the hunt for money to cover the costs of politics. Of these three, the first influences the other two.

It appears that what a democracy needs is a re-examination of its foundations, which should not be betrayed but debated. In addition, it should certainly not be forgotten that being faithful to its own principles does not hinder it from making concessions for the sake of the common good: this is also a form of respect towards opponents and an undoubted way of managing to legislate. Understood in this sense, democracy and compromise – understood here in a way that is decidedly opposed to the acceptance of any position whatsoever – appear to be an indissoluble tandem.

XIV. TOWARDS HYPERDEMOCRACY? THE CRISIS OF LIMITS

Even a superficial observer of history will not fail to grasp the following fact: democracy is not a constant in the historical events of peoples but, rather, and unfortunately, an exception. Certainly, this does not mean that we have to resign ourselves to losing it. On the contrary, we must try to defend it because it is intrinsically fragile. Its weakness depends on the fact, as aeroplane pilots well know, that it has a fatal point of no return which is not, however, easy to identify.

An existentialist philosopher of the twentieth century (Jaspers) argued that the paradox of freedom is that at times it can be lost because of itself. I believe he said: *freedom can be lost by freedom*. Freedom, albeit not always, is not able to protect itself, perhaps because it ends up by ignoring that sense of limits that should characterise it, thereby seeking to absolutise itself. Could this not also be the risk of democracy?

Perhaps we should reflect on the fact that the institutional forms that history has presented us with, and that most draw near to democracy, lasted because that sense of limits that protected them was strongly and decidedly defended.

1. A retrospective look

If we take as examples the Roman republic, the British Commonwealth and American democracy, we see that the mutual division and limitation of powers – which today, as I have already observed, should be updated and broadened – has always impeded the power of the people (or to put it better their representatives) from prevailing over other forms of power. In a few words, true democracy has always refused direct management of the State by the people. Some people argue that in the past such proposals could appear rather fantastic whereas today, thanks to the current prospects held up by ICT, what previously appeared to be a utopia can become reality. There is no need to demonstrate that direct democracy, today as well, constitutes a utopia that – given the instruments that are available – could be even more dangerous.

But although the Roman republic, the British Commonwealth and American democracy today can, specifically as regards the division of powers, appear to be defective given the increased number of power centres that are at work, albeit not always in a controlled and controllable way, in a modern society, in contrary fashion they still have something to tell us about the mechanisms that they were able to set in motion in order to avoid populist negative tendencies.

The formula *Senatus Populusque Romanus* indicated rather well the fundamental role of the people who, called to vote through the *comitia* and guided by its *tribunes*, could even gain access to the consulate. They represented, so to speak, the democratic party, the *populares*, but they were tempered and limited by the aristocratic party of the *patres* present in the Senate.

As the Italian political historians of the Renaissance correctly observed, it is specifically this vivacity of contrasts that brought about the progress of the Roman republic. The democratic party, the *populares*, tended, indeed, on its own, to point to sudden changes because the people, being never satisfied with the results that had been achieved, had an eagerness for almost revolutionary change that was established by real needs, that generated, however, constant instability. In contrary fashion, the aristocratic party of the *patres*, content with its own position and the wellbeing that had been obtained, tended to crystallise society and to put it to sleep in an obtuse reactionary system. The competition of these two parties and their alternation in government – the consuls could never be re-elected – assured the republican miracle. This could be defined as *change in continuity*.

To summarise, the political organism was limited by a balance which imposed a *sense of limits* on each power. This assured the miracle of the long life of the republic which was underpinned by ordinary and extraordinary magistratures – one may think of the two consuls who directed the executive or of the temporary figure of the *dictator* – never since actuated. The republic entered a state of crisis at the point when first the *populares* and then the *patres* came to prevail and crushed their counterpart. What dominated was no longer a sense of limits but (or) the logic of numbers for the *populares* or the logic of force for the *patres*. The attempt at a hyperdemocracy, wanted by the former, was extinguished by the fears of the latter.

To see things correctly, another two modern examples that in terms of duration can compete with the republic of antiquity actuated and defended that sense of limits which made their greatness: the British Commonwealth and American federalism. More than speaking about the first, whose similarities with the Roman system are very numerous, it is helpful to speak about the second and highlight that although it has been a democracy it has hitherto avoided sliding into hyperdemocracy. It has done this specifically by eluding that dangerous logic of numbers so dear to the *populares* and thereby (almost always) avoiding resorting to the logic of violent force beyond the law.

The Americans, even though they did not have an aristocracy tested by history, tried to create the ancient dialogue between the *populares* and the *patres*. We all know that they created two separate chambers and that one of these – and this was no accident – was called the Senate. This last, whose powers are truly notable, does not represent the American people who, as a whole, feel that they are represented by the other chamber. The Senate seems specifically not to take into account the elementary rule of democracy – the rule of numbers. Indeed, the Senate represents the Union of States but it represents them not in a proportional way, as the logical of numbers would require, but by placing them on a level of absolute parity. One State of 30 million electors has the same number of representatives as one that has only 500,000.

To do this, the United States of America took up and dusted down an ancient institution: federalism. This was a pact, as the word indicates, that constitutes an unpassable limit that is able to check the populist negative trends that are a real danger to every democracy. Indeed, federalism constitutes a limitation to the degeneration of democracy only if it places its various parts on a level of real parity. Otherwise, it is masked secessionism, the premiss, which is more or less evident, of democratic unity destined for crisis. That the parts must be placed on a level of parity means in a hypothetical Italian or European federalism that in Italy, notwithstanding the opinion of many people, the representatives of Lombardy or Sicily should count as much as those of Molise and Valle d'Aosta and that in Europe those of Germany and France should count as much as those of Slovenia and Belgium. Perhaps only then could words like solidarity and subsidiarity begin to have a meaning.

2. In praise of representation

Federalism, understood in these terms, constitutes a limitation on the pure and simple law of numbers – the founding criterion for the exponents of various form of direct democracy. This does not only present risks of a technical nature that can be of various kinds but also the risk of eliminating democracy itself. The risks of various kinds range from difficulty in controlling the freedom of those who formulate a judgement to the number of those who actually formulate it. All of this is not enough because it should be borne in mind that judgements are often dictated by the mood of the moment. In this case, politics, as can be easily perceived, would be reduced to a matter of mood with the risk that more than listening to public opinion it would be transformed into a machine for influencing and transforming it. Momentary judgements, by their very nature, would impede that political continuity that is the certain riverbed within which a truly reformist democracy should grow.

There is, however, an even graver risk: that of eliminating democracy itself. To subject everything to the popular will would end up by eliminating one of the greatest achievements of the West – the distinction between the public sphere and the private sphere. The risk of referring everything that concerns the second to the first can generate the unknown of making everything public, everything political, in a word to return to the temptation of a totalitarian democracy whose errors are in front of everyone.

Representative democracy was born specifically as a limitation on the dangerous degeneration of direct democracy. If this last pathway is today in crisis, it should be thought about anew and certainly not abandoned. In addition, representation should also meet a criterion of competence. Some people are delegated to deal with specific questions given that others dedicate themselves to other activities. These last, in a direct democracy, would be constantly distracted from their occupations in order to be concerned with full-time politics. Given that they should represent themselves or anyway be competent to give answers to various questions and issues, their fundamental occupation would certainly suffer as a result, with the dual risk of bringing about, sooner or later, either disenchantment with politics, after it has become too burdensome, or the superficiality of politics.

One then understands why only the rediscovery of 'delegation' would combat the rebirth of populism which still deceives people that it respects the rules of democracy or, worse, behind this populism, the masked appropriation of the direction of politics and support by other powers which today have become undefinable and for this reason cannot be easily limited.

3. The reasons behind the risk of totalitarian democracy

Political progress, like social progress, was based on a growing division of labour and occupations. The triumph of direct democracy compromised this arduous achievement which also generated the achievement of the division of powers. This last, as history has amply demonstrated, disappears when politics is reduced to a pure 'exaggerated belief in assemblies', constant and perennial meetings to discuss constantly and to discuss everything. This continuous exposure to debate ends up by penalising the weakest parts (above all in an emotional sense) of the social fabric. These weakest parts through representation would find a way of being heard. In direct democracy they would run the risk of being suffocated given that they are not able to deal with opposition – often based on verbal violence as well (which is often what happens on the Web) – engaged in by organised groups that are able to ridicule their weakest opponents. In a few words, direct democracy, more than engaging in dialogue with opponents, tends to annihilate them, above all because it seeks to take decisions in a rapid way and to exclude all kinds of mediation. Political choices in this way would end up by being dictated by emotion and improvisation and anyway conditioned by emotionality. We should pay attention to a dilemma that for some time has been troubling the thinkers of recent decades: is totalitarianism a conceptual category linked to a specific historical moment or is it destined to reappear, albeit in different forms?

INDEX OF NAMES

ABETE L., 95
ACKERMAN B., 80, 99-101, 103, 105
ALMOND G.A., 52
AMMIANUS MARCELLINUS, 26
ANDERSON E.N., 131
ANTISERI D., 174-175
ANTONETTI N., 60, 189
ARMELLINI A., 153, 174
AUGUSTINE (ST), 26-27, 70-73, 163, 181
AUSTIN J., 126

BAUMAN Z., 61-62, 73-74, 112-113, 115, 119
BEAUMANOIR F. DE R., 127
BECK U., 111, 142-143
BERLIN I., 21-22, 24, 26, 44, 48, 50, 64, 110-111, 123, 126, 151, 157, 171, 179, 191
BILLIG M., 110
BINGHAM POWELL G., 52
BOBBIO N., 21, 48, 55, 80-81, 85-86, 92, 137-138, 147, 157, 188
BRAUDEL F., 24
BRENNAN J., 75-76
BRYCE J., 122
BURKE E., 67, 78, 100-103, 110, 186
BUTTÀ G., 77

CALVEZ J.Y., 130
CAMPANINI G., 141
CARAMELLA S., 47
CARLYLE R.W., 127
CARROL J., 119
CASSIUS DIO, 34
CHEVALLIER J.J., 127
CIAMPANI A., 97-98
CICERO M.T., 16-17, 70-72, 171, 178

CIPRIANI N., 70, 71, 73
COMPAGNA L., 101, 110, 186
COMPAGNONI F., 132, 188
CORTESE E., 121, 123
COSENTINO F., 54
COTTA M., 80, 127
CRESPI F., 155-156
CRICK B., 59, 64
CUBEDDU R., 100

D'ADDIO M., 13, 39, 102-103, 124
D'AGOSTINO F., 180
DAHL R.A., 149-150, 187
DANTE ALIGHIERI, 42, 121
DAVIDSON D., 176-177
DE GASPERI A., 192
DE RITA G., 95
DIAMANTI I., 84
DI SCIULLO F.M., 77, 145
DONATI P., 156
DUBIEL H., 184
DUMMETT M., 165, 174
DUVERGER M., 82

FALZONE V., 54
FENICHEL PITKIN H., 64, 66-69, 74, 76
FERRAJOLI L., 127-129, 133, 140
FERRARA P., 140, 143, 156
FERRERO G., 134, 193
FRANCO M., 57, 91, 145, 156, 189
FUKUYAMA F., 109

GAIUS, 33, 129
GALIMBERTI U., 168
GAMBINO L., 124, 145, 189
GANDHI M., 43
GAUDEMET J., 24
GIANNINI M.S., 125, 145

GIERKE O., 104
GIULIANI A., 47
GRAZIANO G., 91
GRONCHI G., 48
GUICCIARDINI F., 13, 25, 37, 43
GUTMANN A., 151, 194-195

HABERMAS J., 81, 152-153
HAVEL V., 63
HAYEK VON F.A., 107, 125-126, 135-137
HOBBES T., 64, 101, 110, 124-128, 186, 193
HOPPE H.H., 100, 106
HUNTINGTON S.P., 54

IGNESTI G., 97
INCISA L., 188

JONAS F., 185

KELSEN H., 178
KIMBALL R., 151
KRAUSHAAR W., 184

LEONI B., 103-104
LIVI A., 166, 171
LOEWENSTEIN K., 76
LO PRESTI A., 132
LUCAN L.A., 40, 157

MACIVER R., 148
MALIZIA P., 57
MANIN B., 84, 87
MANN T., 64
MARCHESI C., 54
MARCONI D., 165, 172, 174
MARCUSE H., 55
MARRADI A., 86
MARX K., 55, 130-132, 138, 169, 188
MATTEUCCI N., 55, 80, 85-86, 92, 126, 128, 130, 138, 144, 148, 150, 157, 188
MAZZEI G., 92
MELCHIONNA R., 95
MÉNY Y., 184, 186
MONGARDINI C., 133-134, 143-144

MONTESQUIEU C.L. DE SECONDAT, 16-17, 24, 47-48, 78, 104, 178
MOUNK Y., 109-110
MURA G., 163

NARDONI D., 122
NARDUZZI E., 79, 87-88, 90
NICOLETTI P., 95

OBAMA B., 89
OCCHETTA F., 192

PANEBIANCO A., 80
PALERMO F., 54
PATERNÒ M.P., 153
PASQUINO G., 52, 55, 80, 85-86, 92, 157, 188
PELLICANI L., 162, 194
PEZZIMENTI R., 21, 48, 50, 64, 85, 106, 110-111, 119, 123, 132, 151, 157, 162, 171, 179, 183, 185, 187-188, 191
PIZZORNO A., 64, 67
PITTÈRI D., 89
POPPER K.R., 21, 24, 26, 28, 31, 44, 64, 110-111, 123, 126, 129-132, 151, 157, 168, 171, 175, 179
POSSENTI V., 44, 163-164, 166, 168-169, 174
PUTNAM H., 40, 48, 50, 110, 126, 166-167, 191

QUINTAS A.M., 116

RAWLS J., 134, 137-139, 148-149
ROMANO S., 188
ROSANVALLON P., 59-60, 84, 136
ROSMINI A., 50, 62, 129, 140-142, 180

SANDEL M., 154
SARTORI G., 50, 52
SCHUMPETER J.A., 107
SCOPPOLA P., 97
SEGATORI R., 155-156
SENECA L.A., 25, 41
SERIO M., 48, 52
SIEYÈS E.J., 101-102

SIMMEL G., 113
SPAEMANN R., 35, 179
SPALLETTA M., 93-94
STURZO L., 52-53
SUREL Y., 184, 186-187

TABBONI S., 155
TARCHI M., 184
TAYLOR C., 150-153
THOMPSON D., 194-195
TOCQUEVILLE A. DE, 36-38, 51, 77, 95, 147-148
TOURAINE A., 63, 98, 155
TREU T., 96
TROPER M., 80
TRUFFELLI M., 60, 65

TURALE S., 91
TRUPIA P., 93

URBANI G., 54

VARRO M.T., 70-71
VATTIMO G., 161-162, 171-172, 174-176
VECA S., 21-22, 28, 31, 56, 167

WALZER M., 56,151
WIEVIORKA M., 155
WRIGHT MILLS C., 55
WOLIN S.S., 143

ZAGREBELSKY G., 194
ZAMPETTI P.L., 80, 82-83

www.ingramcontent.com/pod-product-compliance
Lightning Source LLC
Chambersburg PA
CBHW032253150426
43195CB00008BA/432